ABOUT THE

Sheridan 'Shed' Si[...]
entrepreneurial ma[...]
a global novelty gift empire (including
products such as the 'Sergeant Pepper Mill',
'The Sound Machine' and the 'Control-
A-Man' and 'Control-A-Woman' remote
controls), been a renowned TV Producer
(*Big Brother*, *The Big Breakfast*, *Space
Cadets*), is the bestselling author of *Presents
Money Can't Buy* and *Ideas Man*, and a
corporate speaker on success, creativity and
innovation, among other achievements.

Some of Shed's ideas include a range of novelty products,
which have sold over a million units worldwide, a ground-
breaking documentary that involved him going undercover
as a sixteen-year-old schoolboy (when he was thirty) and
the launch of his own currency – the 'EGO'. He also made
publishing history by becoming the first person ever to get
a totally blank book into the top fifty of Amazon's bestseller
chart, when he published *What Every Man Thinks About
Apart From Sex* – a book with two hundred completely blank
pages. It has since been translated around the world.

Shed's ability to create new ideas matched with his skill to make
them happen means that his range and rate of success is huge.

www.ShedSimove.com

WELCOME

SUCCESS... OR YOUR MONEY BACK

The Quickest Success Manual Ever That Shows You
HOW TO GET ANYTHING YOU DESIRE...

SHED SIMOVE

HAY HOUSE

HAY HOUSE
Australia • Canada • Hong Kong • India
South Africa • United Kingdom • United States

THIRTY SECRETS

FIRST OFF...I WILL NOW READ YOUR MIND

Hello, my name is Shed. I know that might sound a bit odd, but it's what my parents called me from an early age (it's short for 'Sheridan'). So that's that, and great to be with you.

One of my huge drives in life is to come up with new ideas and then make them happen. Right now though, my only focus is YOU. My aim is to make this book incredibly useful to you – and hopefully entertaining and interesting as well. You'll soon judge whether I succeed…

First though, I'm going to read your mind. So, prepare to be astonished. Okay, good…hold still…it's coming through.

The fact that you're reading this book tells me so much about you. To start with, it tells me that you're someone who *wants* to make things happen. Second, you're someone who searches for information about *how* to make things happen. Already, these two facts about you mean that you've got all the necessary skills for success in any field you want: namely, you've got both the desire to succeed and also the intelligence to search for ways to make that success come to life. And that's something wonderful to confirm about yourself, isn't it?

In this book, my aim is to remind you how amazing your brain is and to get you both excited and inspired about what it can do, by sharing powerful secrets that'll hopefully dispel any doubts you may have about yourself (because we all have many) and by delivering solid techniques for achieving anything you desire. Quite a bold proposition for a short book then but, hey, it's always good to aim high. So here we go...

SECRET 1
EVERYONE IS A CHARLATAN

The first secret is wonderfully comforting and although no one shares it when you're growing up, they most certainly should. It's an all-encompassing secret, which reassures you that…

ANYONE (AND THAT MEANS YOU AND I, TOO) CAN MAKE IT BIG

I discovered this secret later on in my life and I wish someone had told me earlier. For me, one of my biggest life-changing epiphanies occurred after I'd been living in the world for a fair while – around age thirty, in fact. It took me that long to realise this very simple fact:

ALL ADULTS ARE BLUFFING IT

As I watched some very successful people around me (in order to learn from them and work out how they made things happen), it became more and more obvious that every single person I studied was pretty much making it up as they went along, every single day. I'd previously thought that successful people had some sort of magical power or secret plan, which made them better than others, but I quickly came to realise that people who succeed are very much like everyone else, except in one area:

THEY TRY THINGS

Now, you might say…*'That's nonsense! Surely success is about knowledge?'*

And I'd reply, *'Yes, knowledge can often be an important factor when achieving something you desire.'* However the great thing about knowledge is that it's very easily found (both from the people around you and, incredibly these days, from the internet) and it can then be easily planted into your brain. All you have to do is find it and absorb it – perfect!

But what you *can't* go out and find in a book or on the web are the *qualities* that will make you succeed – powerful traits like drive and chutzpah. And the main point of this book is to show you that *no matter* how much (or little) knowledge someone has, none of us will ever make it – unless we…

GIVE SOMETHING A GO

It's worth remembering that anyone who tries a new idea *has* to – by very definition – 'bluff it'. If you're doing something that has never been done before, then there's most definitely not going to be a plan or blueprint for you to follow. It's a complete 'hit-and-hope' situation. The important point is just to start hitting and hoping. And your natural judgement and inbuilt capacity to learn will pull you through from then on.

Most people who are deemed 'successful' are simply making the very best of what small talent they have. Of course, some successful people in the world do have a huge amount of a specific exceptional raw talent, but they're in the minority, and even they had to make thousands of mistakes before their skills really shone out. Most successful men and women have simply taken steps to maximise a tiny amount of potential by constantly honing and perfecting one specific area of their talent until it grew. Then, they always surround themselves with good people who can help them to exploit that talent.

So, never ever worry that you're not good enough to make something happen.

YOU ARE

It's also helpful to keep in mind that no one is perfect. That's what makes us all interesting. Every single person – no matter how clever, beautiful, skilled or confident they are – makes mistakes and has problems.

Let's just get that really clear: no one (not even so-called 'famous and successful' people like Richard Branson, James Dyson or Donald Trump) has all the answers. Often

Everyone is a Charlatan

these so-called 'geniuses' hire people to help them or they make massive mistakes before they hit the big time and they simply learn from them. Success, in any area of life, is all about *decisions.*

And, just like all highly successful people, you are perfectly capable of making decisions (after all, you make hundreds every day about lots of things). The only difference is that the decisions you make today are slightly different to the ones you'll be making when you try something new. But they still require you to go through exactly the same process that you use every day, already!

For example, if you have to decide what to have for lunch then you'll probably weigh up all the available options and use your best judgement, listen to your gut feeling (sometimes a 'hungry-gut' feeling if it's to do with lunch) and then you'll decide.

And you'll use the same principle with anything you try. Once you decide to start a new venture, you just have to plough on, making choices that feel right to you – and you'll be on your way to becoming just like anyone you aspire to be. I can tell you this so confidently because the logic of it is very simple – either you'll get something right first time...or you'll learn how to get it right the second, third or fourth time. So, as long as you start doing something new and stick with it for a while, it's a guaranteed win-win situation.

SECRET 2
THE FOUR WORDS YOU MUST GET USED TO

Whether you're trying to get something done on your own (for either business or pleasure) or you're part of a team in a company, there are four words that will always crop up during your journey to success. Because you'll definitely hear these words, it's very useful to build your own personal mental armour to deal with them. The first of these words is...

'NO!'

And the other three are...

'IT'LL NEVER WORK!'

Now, all these words must be treated with the respect they deserve – that is, VERY LITTLE. Whenever you come up with a new idea that you want to put into practice, you may well hear these utterances from friends, relatives and colleagues – and you must be very aware of the power they wield and, crucially, not let that power deter you from your path to success. Sometimes, when I face a wall of rejection or negativity, I surf the net looking for examples of people who were told *'NO, IT'LL NEVER WORK'* and who, after persevering, went on to achieve huge success, simply because they never gave up.

When I was trying to get my first 'proper' book *Ideas Man* published, I received dozens and dozens of rejection letters from literary agents and publishers. Huge doubts started to creep into my mind that perhaps I should give up. So, to spur myself on (because often it's up to you to motivate yourself), I went on the web and found out that some huge names in publishing had also encountered many rejections before they made it. Something curious happens whenever you encounter someone that you or others deem 'successful' – namely, you don't usually know how many times, or for how long, they were *not successful* before they 'made it'.

For example, ex-lawyer turned writer John Grisham tried to get a deal for his first book, *A Time to Kill*, and was rejected by fifteen publishers and thirty agents. It went on to sell millions of copies worldwide. The modern classic *Animal Farm* by George Orwell was also turned down by publishers in both the U.S. and U.K. One publisher even remarked that, *'It is impossible to sell animal stories in the U.S.A.'* When it was finally published, Orwell's story became one of the most important books in recent history. Even J.K. Rowling of Harry Potter fame got knocked back nine times (how sick must those publishers feel now!) before someone spotted the book's potential.

All these examples made me feel better when I was first starting out, because I saw how even 'the greats' had major setbacks and show you that it's always worth ploughing on and, in fact, vital to do so. So that's exactly what I did with my first book, and though it took a while, eventually a publisher recognised the book's potential and took me on.

Here's a remarkable thought: it's much easier to find reasons why something WON'T work than reasons why it will.

'WHY?'

Maybe it's a part of the human condition to find problems quickly. The ability to speedily recognise threats and dangers helped us when we lived in the wild. So, perhaps that's why we find it easy to spot 'danger' or problems up ahead when considering any plan to make something happen. Luckily, it's also a unique ability of the amazing brain in our heads to be able to come up with wonderfully creative solutions to overcome any problems too. Because you're human, that means you're programmed to find solutions.

So, it's important to remember that there will always be dozens and dozens of reasons that people around you (and even you, yourself) will come up with 'excuses' for why a new idea won't work. It's your very important job to avoid letting these reasons dissuade you from your path and instead focus on working out all the ways your plan *can* work and then go on to prove to yourself and others around you that it *does* work.

No matter how many setbacks or knockbacks you get, it's absolutely vital that…

YOU MUST KEEP BELIEVING IN YOURSELF
– AND YOUR IDEA –
AND CARRY ON

Of course, you can (and should) listen to other people's feedback, because it may give you pointers for adjusting your strategy so that you obtain success even more quickly. I'll explain more about this exciting method in a secret coming up later.

For now though, all you have to do is take comfort from the fact that when times are hard and success looks like it'll never happen, you must remember if you're hearing *'No'*, *'It'll never work'* – or *even* the four words *'You can't do that…'* – first, you're in good company and, second, you're most certainly on the right track to success. These responses all signify that you're starting to make something happen and only by *starting* will you ever succeed.

SECRET 3
THE AMAZING W.C.S. SYSTEM

Whenever my internal demons chatter at me and cast doubts over whether I can attain a big ambition, I use a simple system that really helps me to move forward. Maybe it'll work for you, too.

When you're having doubts about trying something new, ask yourself this:

'WHAT IS THE VERY WORST THAT CAN HAPPEN IN THIS SITUATION?'

This question is the core of my W.C.S. (which stands for 'Worst Case Scenario') system. It's designed to get myself off my backside and spur me on to start making an idea happen. By asking yourself one simple question before you attempt any new ambition – *'What's the worst thing that can happen if I start trying to reach this goal?'* – you not only force your mind to consider the risks of pursuing this path (and if they're too high, then you can decide to stop, and if they're not, you'll feel instantly relieved that you can just begin on your journey), plus you'll also be mentally prepared for any challenges you face on the way.

Years ago, I became gripped with the desire to create and launch a 'novelty gift' – the kind of product you might see on a shop shelf that's fun, not too expensive and something you might buy someone for a quick present. I had absolutely no experience in this area, having previously worked in the T.V. industry.

As you know, the fear of failure can be mightily powerful – it's a force that takes over your whole body and mind – and often stops most people (but not us!) from starting anything unfamiliar. I was determined to reach my goal, so I employed the W.C.S. system and just asked myself: *'What's the worse thing that can happen?'*

The answers I came up with were:

*   Novelty gift companies would hate my concepts and I'd be laughed out of their offices.

*   I might realise that I simply wasn't good at coming up with novelty gift ideas.

*   My friends, family – and colleagues – would know I'd failed.

*   I could lose some of my hard-earned savings.

And so on…

But then I thought: *'Well, all these terrible scenarios are scary – and certainly not ideal – but I definitely could get through them if they happened…Yes, they'd be slightly traumatic perhaps (get the "shrink" on standby), but certainly not life threatening.'*

So, once I've mentally checked that any new goal I'm going to tackle won't ruin my life if it goes any other way than my dream outcome, I set myself a manageable task.

I do this because it's very important to break your long-term goal into shorter achievable tasks because then the long-term goal doesn't seem so overwhelming. It's incredibly helpful to set yourself a goal that you know you can reach reasonably soon.

So, I set myself the short-term goal of getting just two meetings with different novelty gift companies and to pitch them three ideas each. It's always good to pitch more than one idea in any meeting as it gives you options if your first idea is instantly knocked back for whatever reason. I told myself that if, after these two meetings, I hadn't managed to persuade any of the companies to make one of my ideas, then I'd either call it a day (which isn't actually what you must do, but reassuring yourself like this is a very useful psychological crutch because it removes the pressure to complete the whole task all at once and also gets you into the powerfully helpful frame of mind where you remind yourself that simply *trying* something will mean you'll have achieved your aim) or that after the two meetings I'd come up with some more ideas.

At the first meeting, I went in, pitched my concepts and the company boss virtually laughed me out the door, and not in a good way. It was horrible and soul-destroying. All my ideas got rejected outright. And the second was rough too. '*No thanks, Shed*' came the quick reply.

I didn't give up. Over the next months, I scheduled three more meetings. But the same thing kept happening over and over. All the company bosses knocked my ideas back outright.

The curious thing about getting many '*NOs*' is that you always learn from them. This is vital to remember. The '*NOs*' you sometimes encounter (and *frequently* encounter, in my case!) actually help you to reach your goal, albeit later than you'd hoped. These '*NOs*' also can have the effect of spurring you on, and forcing you to make your pitch much better next time.

I began to examine *why* I was getting knocked back and started to suspect that it wasn't my ideas that were getting rejected (both I, and friends and family members I respected, firmly believed they had merit) but instead, it was *me* who was being rejected. And one reason I thought this was happening was that I was an outsider, with no track record in the novelty gift industry. But how was I supposed to get in, if no one would give me a chance?

This is a common problem that many people encounter when they're starting out to pursue a new goal: the fact that you've had no success in the past means no one will back you or partner with you to create success in the future. It's a hugely frustrating vicious circle. So you must – and definitely can – break it.

At times like this, you need to take the bull (and the rest of the herd) firmly by the horns and…

HARNESS SOME OF THE 'I'LL SHOW YOU!' EMOTIONAL DRIVE INSIDE YOU

In my case, I firmly tapped into my *'I'll show you!'* drive and decided to change tack as well. In order to get companies to partner with me, I figured I needed to prove to them that one of my ideas could be successful in the gift market. Ironically, this would mean I'd have to manufacture and launch a novelty product myself. It took me a while, but after searching for a factory on the internet, I found a manufacturer in China and commissioned them to make a new range of saucy confectionery that I'd recently dreamed up. It was a tough process, but possible. I had to create all the designs and artwork for the candy myself, sort out the shipping and distribution – plus scrabble together my savings to make the whole thing happen. But eventually, I triumphed. I shipped across thousands of packets of my confectionery and found a buyer for them.

Months later, my range of candy had completely sold out. Then, a wonderful thing happened. I suddenly began to receive calls from the companies who'd previously rejected all my ideas. They'd seen that one of my concepts was a great seller in the novelty market – and so now they wanted to partner with me and bring some of my ideas to life. It was a case of taking two steps back (tackling the hard task of making the confectionery by myself) in order to take the two steps forward – of being allowed the privilege of partnering with a company who already had huge industry expertise and thus could sell many more units than I could distribute on my own.

And now, many years later, I work with lots of different novelty companies and I've sold more than a million novelty gifts worldwide. As you know, this was after coming to the industry with absolutely no experience of it at all.

By using the W.C.S. system, and imagining the absolute worst case scenario of humiliation, embarrassment and rejection, I braced myself for setbacks, so that when they arrived (and I did have some truly awful meetings) it wasn't so much of a bone-crushing shock and that meant I was able to bounce back much more easily.

This technique might seem to fly in the face of the traditional 'positive thinking only' school of thought, but it's far more useful when you're deciding whether to start making a new idea happen because it deals with the internal doubts we all have. Rather than blindly telling yourself *'everything will be all right'*, instead this technique reassures you that, *'everything might not be all right, but as long as you've considered how things might not go as planned, and decided that you could deal with those outcomes, then the way ahead is wonderfully clear for you to start making your new target happen…'*

In short, when you're considering whether to try to achieve any new goal, if you use the W.C.S. system to project forward and imagine how things could *possibly* go badly wrong, then this will allow you to check whether the risks are too high. If you decide that they are, then of course you shouldn't go ahead – but often they won't be. Plus, by mentally projecting events into the future in order to consider the downsides of embarking on something new, this will also mean you get to manage any fears that may arise from starting that journey (because it's certainly daunting to begin chasing a new goal – and it's simply normal to feel that way). Once you've neutered at least some of the demons that EVERYONE naturally has, you can take the first step and push forward to success.

SECRET 4
THEY LIED TO YOU

This secret isn't taught in schools, but it really should be.

In classes around the world, most pupils are given a diet of traditional fare (learning individual 'subjects') instead of being educated in the far more useful skill of…

HOW TO BE A SUCCESSFUL HUMAN BEING

Now, I'm a strong believer that any knowledge you put into your brain is beneficial (both because it gives you expertise in that new area and also because it will *always* shape your future ideas and how you implement them), so I'm not saying we should stop giving students the option to study anything they wish, more that I firmly believe 'personal development' needs to be something compulsory for everyone. We should all learn how to become fulfilled, decent members of society who are easily capable of making our dreams come true.

Instead of learning 'techniques for success', most people grow up with snippets of information gleaned from common knowledge. The problem is that these snippets don't often deliver the whole truth about the process of how to achieve any goal you might have, and sometimes even *make it seem like something to avoid*.

Here's one such snippet you'll most certainly have heard:

IF AT FIRST YOU DON'T SUCCEED
TRY AND TRY AGAIN

Well, we need to add a few more words onto the end of that quote, to make it slightly more helpful:

IF AT FIRST YOU DON'T SUCCEED
TRY AND TRY AGAIN

BUT IF YOU'VE TRIED MANY TIMES
WITHOUT SUCCESS

THEN YOU MUST CHANGE YOUR STRATEGY!

Persistence is, quite simply, not enough. Instead, what you need to do is persist *and evolve* your approach to success. 'Never giving up' is fine (and necessary), but simply doing the same thing again and again may well only deliver the same results, and that's why you must frequently change your approach or – even better – try lots of different strategies at the same time. By creating lots of eggs in your 'opportunities basket', you'll have a much greater chance that one will 'hatch' into success…(That's enough of the egg analogies for now.)

The successful writer and playwright Samuel Beckett also had his own version of this idea. He said:

'Try again. Fail again. Fail better.'

That's inspiring isn't it! In saying 'Fail better' Beckett neatly forces your brain to re-understand that 'failing' is something necessary, beneficial and worth striving for.

Exactly.

Here's a thought that comforts me when I encounter a 'setback' or 'challenge' (much better words than 'failure'):

**A 'FAILURE' IS
SIMPLY SOMETHING
THAT TELLS YOU
THAT YOU'RE ONE STEP NEARER
TO YOUR GOAL**

Here's another big tip for success:

**ONE WORD YOU MUST BANISH
FROM YOUR VOCABULARY...**

That word is...

LUCK

Because when it comes to success in life...

THERE IS NO SUCH THING AS 'LUCK'

The truth of the matter is quite different – and actually should make you feel incredibly empowered. The fact is that...

NOTHING HAPPENS WITHOUT YOU MAKING IT HAPPEN

'Luck' is often used as an excuse by people who don't want to try to attain success or by people who want to give up. These people might say: *'Other people are far luckier than me'* or they say *'My luck has run out and so I can't reach my goal.'*

Nonsense!

These attitudes are very dangerous because they suggest that your life is controlled by external factors that are uncontrollable by you.

Well I'm here to tell you different:

1. 'LUCK' IS A MYTH

And...

2. YOU CAN CONTROL PRETTY MUCH ANYTHING

The human race has put a man on the moon (if you don't believe it was a hoax, of course!), cured many diseases and even created impressive innovations, such as the electric blanket (lovely for your grandma). All these feats are amazing achievements, and show us that...

ANYTHING IS POSSIBLE

Rather than waiting for 'luck' to happen to us, each of us must realise that *only we* are responsible for what happens in our life. The key is to take control and create situations that allow 'good things' (or *'lucky things'* as some people wrongly call them) to happen.

So the concept of 'being lucky' is a falsehood. You can only put yourself in situations that make you 'lucky'.

When I made some of my first gift products, a big firm in the U.S.A. asked me to develop another product that went on to sell more than the original product I'd sold them.

This happened when I released a novelty item called 'The Parent–Child Contract Pad' (a simple notepad that mimics a formal contract for adults and kids to fill in) and the buyers at the U.S. gift chain told me that they wanted another item to sit next to the pad on their shelves and have even broader appeal. I quickly suggested an idea to the fantastic partner company I was working with at the time, and we went on to release the 'Sound Machine' (a little plastic box that plays sixteen different sounds, from applause to explosions – and even burping). It went on to be a surprise hit around the world.

Was that lucky? Fortunate, perhaps – yes. But actually, that example of success wasn't down to 'luck', it was down to the fact that I'd created a product in the first place that gave me the chance to be 'lucky' in the future.

So, it's good to always remember…

**SUCCESSFUL PEOPLE AREN'T 'LUCKY',
THEY SIMPLY CREATE OPPORTUNITIES
FOR GREAT THINGS TO HAPPEN**

SECRET 5
WHY YOU'LL SOON FIND OTHER PEOPLE'S SWEAT *WILDLY* ATTRACTIVE

Thomas Edison, the hugely successful American inventor of the light bulb (and many other amazing inventions, including the camera and the record player) famously failed many, many times before he succeeded, and he once said:

> *'Genius is one per cent inspiration and ninety-nine per cent perspiration.'*

This quote is used by everyone – from teachers to parents to work colleagues.

Now, we all know that a large measure of success is most definitely down to the dogged and relentless pursuit of a goal – 'hard work', as it's commonly known. This is, of course, rather annoying, because it would be wonderful if achieving any success was an effortless process. Well, unfortunately it's not. However, the better news is that you can most certainly take shortcuts to make success happen much more easily and way more quickly.

Edison's belief that the process to attain success is mostly made up of 'perspiration' is indeed accurate, if a little daunting, but fantastically there's some brilliant shining light at the end of that slightly frustrating tunnel:

IT DOESN'T HAVE TO BE *YOUR* PERSPIRATION

When you look at highly successful people, it might seem as if they've got a certain extra skill that other people just don't have. What no one tells you is that none of these people do it alone. In order to be successful, there's no doubt that on some scale you must be a good leader, but in reality, all this means is that you need the ability to make good decisions and communicate your ideas clearly. Then, other people will work with you. And you can learn both of these skills if you haven't got them already (which all of us have to some degree).

It's an obvious, but perhaps important fact to remember that...

NO PERSON CAN ATTAIN SUCCESS ALONE

You can (and must) 'delegate' or 'partner' with, talented people.

That is, you must find people to work with you who can help you reach your goal. You can do this in two ways:

either by paying others to work with you (the conventional route), or by persuading people to work with you by using some other reward. And I don't mean sleep with them! (Although…if it works for you…then go for your life!)

As long as you bring some value to the party, whether it's your visionary ideas, communication skills or even that you're simply a lovely person to be around, then it'll be much more likely that someone will work with you, because having any of these traits will help get things done.

Working with others and delegating tasks has been the key factor in every successful person's rise to the top. And, actually, the basic way the capitalist world works is…

(SHOCK HORROR! HOLD THE FRONT PAGE!)

…to pay workers less than the value of what they produce.

Outrageous, eh! Now, let's all become communists or live on a kibbutz.

Or, maybe not…

The difference between the value that a worker creates and the value they're paid is simply how 'profit' is created. That's the way society works in the Western world at the moment. Of course, there are always ways to make this arrangement less starkly 'exploitative'. For example, a much kinder – and softer – model is to give workers performance bonuses or shares in the business, so as the success of the company grows, the workers share in this success, too.

But the good news is that in order to succeed at anything you do, while the 'inspiration' is likely to be yours, the 'perspiration' doesn't have to be.

IN FACT, YOU SHOULD USE
AS LITTLE OF YOUR PERSPIRATION AS POSSIBLE

This will then free you up to have even more inspiration and thus build more teams and embark upon lots more successful ventures. So it's incredibly helpful to…

FIND EXPERTS TO HELP YOU

It's always best to work with people around you who are experts in their areas, or better than you at some specific skill. This is sometimes hard to do because when you're the leader, it's common to feel the need to be the most skilled person on the project. But actually, listening to your partners and team, so that you can make great decisions, is all that matters. People who are more talented than you in a certain area will stay with you if: a) you treat them well (both on a human level and also in a business way); and b) you keep making good decisions that ultimately lead them to being fulfilled, recognised and rewarded.

There's another famous phrase that's used a lot when people are talking about 'succeeding':

PEOPLE SAY SUCCESS IS OFTEN ABOUT 'WHO YOU KNOW'

NOW, THIS IS OFTEN ACCURATE

BUT 'NOT KNOWING' THE RIGHT PEOPLE SHOULD NEVER BE USED AS A REASON NOT TO START SOMETHING.

THIS IS YET ANOTHER EXCUSE FOR NOT TRYING TO MAKE AN IDEA COME TO LIFE

Not every successful person is born 'knowing' the people that matter! And if you're one of the people (like myself) who doesn't know lots of people in lots of industries, then you simply need to think about how to meet – and more importantly, impress – the crucial people you want to work with, and then they'll team up with you.

The secret to meeting experts...

These days, experts, who can help you achieve any goal, can be found at the click of a mouse. But, sometimes, it might be hard to actually connect with these experts over the internet, as they're very busy people who often receive a lot of random emails. These messages might well be tough for them to wade through and so it could prove harder to get yourself noticed via email. However, some experts can indeed be contacted this way, so it's always worth a try.

Another technique I've found to be highly useful when finding experts to help you with your goals is to attend TRADE SHOWS. These are events where experts all come together under one roof, making it easy for you to meet many of them in one spot at one time. Powerful! And you can often easily sign up for trade shows on the web.

Now, I usually attend trade shows on the last day, because by that time most of the exhibitors will have already had most of their important meetings, meaning they'll be more relaxed and likely to engage with a stranger like you or me. Once I arrive, I stand back and watch the different stallholders, carefully seeing how they operate, what their products or services are like, if they're friendly to people who approach them and if, generally, I get a great feeling both about them and what they do. If I do, I then politely introduce myself and quickly ask for their business card.

It's important to remember that anyone who has a stand at a trade fair is mainly in 'selling' mode, so the last thing they want to do is get engaged in 'buying', which is what you're essentially asking them to do if you're pitching your ideas to them. So, I absolutely don't 'cold pitch' at a trade fair, I simply make it my goal to get a business card that allows me to contact the company at a later date. Then, around two weeks after the fair (when the company will have dealt with a lot of the orders and meetings arising from the fair), I email or call them and explain where we met. By mentioning you crossed paths at the recent trade fair, it marks you out as being a little more serious about their area of expertise, an insider almost, and not just another random enquiry.

Then I ask whether they ever work with partners. If they do, and they're interested in meeting me as a possible future partner, I arrange a date to visit them at their premises (you can tell a lot about a company from their offices and team) and then pitch my ideas to them.

'W.I.I.F.M.' and 'W.I.I.F.T.'

It's easy to work out *'What's in it for me?'* when you meet an expert and ask them to help bring your idea to life. The acronym 'W.I.I.F.M.' always makes me chuckle because it's rather vulgar in a way but, actually, when you're trying to get an expert to help you, you need to think 'W.I.I.F.T.' – *'What's in it for them?'* This is because unless you're offering something they haven't got, then there's no reason they'll disrupt their busy work schedule to bring you into the fold. Experts in their field often have lots on their plate and frequently run successful businesses, so if you want to get their help or to partner with them, it's completely VITAL you show that you can bring value to their life – and business – in some way.

That's why your ideas must be really good – and original too. Always check beforehand that anything you're going to pitch doesn't already exist in the market or, if it does, that your version is sufficiently different to the ideas that have been launched before, or even that the idea is ripe to be reinvented. You can do this via a simple search on the net.

Plus, when you go to meet someone to pitch to them initial very early-stage ideas, you should always, *always*, *always*, *always* (have I conveyed how important I think this is yet?)…

BRING *MORE THAN ONE IDEA* TO THE EXPERT YOU WANT TO WORK WITH

This is because your first idea might be something that's not quite right for them, it might be something they've genuinely already thought of, or it might be something they're currently developing already. These are all completely valid explanations as to why the person you're pitching to, won't (or can't) take your idea forward – and they've all been given to me numerous times. It's at this point you need to be able to say, *'No problem, how about this next idea then…'* and launch into your next pitch.

Another reason why you *must* take lots of ideas to your initial pitch meeting is because of the way people are built psychologically. Every single one of us likes to feel special, valuable – and respected. And so, when you go to anyone for help, and especially an expert in their field, you must give them the opportunity to show you they have value. In order to pitch successfully, you need to clearly demonstrate to the other person that you actively care about their opinions and advice. And actually, this is only polite too.

Even though it might seem odd, bringing someone a solution that is totally and utterly formed might not always be the best way. When you're pitching, it's likely that you won't have a complete 'route to success' fully solved anyway – that's why you're asking for help or a partner. But, the fact remains that...

YOU SHOULD BOTH LOOK FOR, AND EXPECT, FEEDBACK AND ADVICE FROM THE PERSON YOU'RE PITCHING TO

And you can – and should – do this in two main ways.

FIRST, by presenting more than one idea – whether it's in a business meeting or when you're trying to get something done with a loved one – you instantly show the other person that you respect they *should* have a choice in deciding between ideas and also that you're happy to empower them to make that choice. Most of us humans need to feel we have 'worth', and by allowing someone to make choices (and sometimes, even letting them shoot certain options down in flames) we give them authority over the proceedings, and show them that what they think (or do) has an effect. This way, they get to show you they are 'valuable'. As well as respecting the dynamic between you, by letting the expert chew your idea around in the meeting, you'll often get feedback that will be highly useful to you. By listening to the expert and allowing them to discuss your idea, you can pick up exactly what they're looking for at that time, and thus be able to pitch again another time even more successfully.

SECOND, as well as giving choices to someone you're pitching to, it's also absolutely vital that you leave some room for their suggestions, not only because their feedback may well be useful and enhance your finished idea amazingly well – or give you ideas for future concepts – but also because it immediately shows them that you respect their input and will continue to do so if they partner with you. When I say 'give an expert room', I mean that (once you've shown them an idea) you should let the other person say what they think, then pause and ask a question or two. Often, the expert you're meeting will add something fantastic to your idea, making it even more attractive and easier to get off the ground.

But, even if the other person says they hate your idea, or they tell you that 'IT'LL NEVER WORK', you should resist the (natural) urge to go on the defensive right away by immediately explaining why you created your idea like you did – or even, why they're completely wrong!

Sometimes, a person's first reaction on hearing an idea is not really what they think deep down, it's just a snap decision having seen or heard your idea for the first time. And sometimes, even a really clever person will feel the need simply to respond immediately in some way, and then (if you allow them) will proceed to talk themselves round in a circle, ending up with an idea pretty much exactly as you first suggested! It's just the way people often are, so it's super important for you to be calm, attentive and to let the expert think aloud.

These interactions happen because of the innate human need to want to 'contribute' and be 'useful'. After you've pitched to someone who initially tells you your idea is terrible, or that it won't work, once you've given them room and a little time to think about it more clearly, they might well come to another conclusion – and often, it might even be the one that you presented in the first place.

Therefore, when you suggest an idea to someone you want to work with and they say anything about your idea, how you react is a bit like a test. If you react in a measured way and ask some more questions to clarify precisely what the other person is thinking (and make it easy for them to give more input), then explain your thought processes, this will show the other person that you're willing to listen when they talk and also that you want to understand their point of view (vital to them when deciding whether they want to work with you). It also gives them room to see you've thought things through and gives them time to change their mind. Of course, sometimes you might change yours too. It's important to have a clear vision for your idea, but at the start of making an idea happen, it's also important to know that in order to make it happen...

YOU SHOULD BE FLEXIBLE AND OPEN TO STRATEGIES, WHICH COULD MAKE IT EVEN BETTER

I've been in lots of meetings where the person I'm pitching to makes a (negative) snap decision about one of my ideas, but after I've asked some more questions and given them my thought processes about how the idea came to be, they've then completely changed their view and said my original idea could work well. On many other occasions, I've gone to meet someone with ideas that I thought were fully formed and totally great, and the other person has made suggestions which completely enhanced each concept, making the final products way better than I'd originally envisaged them.

Whenever you're attempting to partner with anyone who has more expertise than you, as well as giving them more than one option (for both practical and emotional reasons), and room for them to suggest changes and updates, there's another important key to getting them to team up with you.

If you want an expert to help you, you have to offer them something they don't already have, and this can be the idea you present, or the contribution you make that'll help bring the idea to life – or even, both. By always thinking *'What can I offer the other party…'* and making sure you take steps to answer that question well, you'll ensure you're superbly prepared for any meetings and set up for success.

Now, once you're in a pitch, the best way to bring your idea to life is to use a method that cuts out some work for the person you're pitching to. This is exceptionally vital.

YOU MUST BRING YOUR IDEAS TO LIFE

Nurture your nuggets

Once you bring your idea to life (more than simply storing it your head or as a line in a notebook), you'll both communicate your idea much more effectively, and you'll also make it way harder for people to snuff your idea out. Furthermore, presenting your idea as a simple graphic, 3-D model or crude prototype makes it far easier for people around you to suggest helpful ways to get it done. You don't need a big budget to bring an idea to life, there's *always* a cheap way of proving an idea. You just have to find it.

EVEN A BIG IDEA CAN BE BOILED DOWN TO ITS PUREST ELEMENTS

Let's say your goal is to make a movie. A pretty big task, you might think? Well, if you're passionate about making a movie, then shoot one or two scenes on a cheap video camera and edit it on a computer – at least you'll then be able to show that the story and the characters are gripping. This will help you persuade the experts who can make the movie happen that you're really serious about your goal and you'll have the energy and initiative to see it through to completion, crucial factors for them to know, especially if they're pouring their own money into making your idea happen.

When I first began pitching gift and novelty ideas, I disciplined myself in a couple of ways that became key strategies to getting my ideas off the ground.

First, I trained myself to ruthlessly write my ideas down as soon as I had them (something you have to do, and I still do today). By doing this, I started to create a portfolio of ideas. I used a simple Word document on my computer and then wrote the title for each idea at the top in clear, large type. There was no special technical knowledge needed to do this, which was very fortunate because I don't have any.

Then the other way I ensured that my ideas would have a chance at coming to fruition was to communicate all my concepts by bringing them to life in a very crude way. This was also done at no cost and with no special software skills either. You'd think that to be able to design new products, you'd need to be a designer with fancy Photoshop skills. Wrong! In order to communicate any idea, I use any relevant images I find on the internet and stick them together on a page, plus I often use Clip Art too – the pre-made, line-drawn graphics, which are also freely available all over the web. All you need to do is bring an idea to life to the point where the person looking at it can get the core concept and then begin to visualise how it *could* be. This makes it much easier for them to make a decision as to whether it's something exciting they'd want to be involved with.

When I pitched my range of novelty remote controls called 'Control-A-Man' and 'Control-A-Woman', I showed prospective partners images of real remote controls with ideas for new buttons underneath, like 'TALK ABOUT FEELINGS' on the 'Control-A-Man' and 'REMOVE CLOTHES' for the 'Control-A-Woman' (these suggestions neatly reflected my view that women are far more layered than men). The very basic visuals I presented brought the idea to life just enough so that anyone I showed them to could instantly see what the potential of the idea could be. Fortunately, the first company boss I showed them to had a brilliant mind and got the concept right away. And, together, we went on to sell more than a quarter of a million novelty remote controls.

These days, I use the internet to find amazing designers who can bring my designs to life quickly, which means it doesn't cost too much to communicate any concept professionally, powerfully and beautifully. And, if you have no budget at all, you could always persuade a designer to help you by agreeing to cut them in on the deal when you start getting income in, down the line.

Sometimes when you work with a designer, their design comes out so well that it allows a factory, or the experts you're working with, to be able to skip a step in the design process. And that means that what you've brought them has even more value.

You can also make a prototype yourself if it's not too hard. This is easier if you're making a novelty gift as opposed to a ground-breaking new car, but the principle is the same:

BRING YOUR IDEA TO LIFE IN SOME WAY OTHER THAN A THOUGHT IN YOUR HEAD, AND INSTANTLY IT GAINS MASSIVE POWER

When I wanted to get a publisher for my first 'gift book' called *Presents Money Can't Buy* (which was all about thoughtful things you can do for others), I did a doodle for each concept in the book, then got a mock-up of the book printed at a local printer and relentlessly sent these crude prototypes to publishers. I got dozens and dozens of rejections, year after year, but the publisher who eventually decided to work with me liked my doodles so much that they kept them in the final book.

Anything you can do to help to bring your idea to life and persuade an expert to partner with you, so much the better. And when you have great people working with you, absolutely anything is possible.

NO SWEAT!

SECRET 6
YOU MUST BE 'THE EVOLVING CHAMELEON'

Here's another secret that's almost so beautiful in its simplicity that it should be called a work of art and placed in the LOUVRE.

This secret comes in three steps and is as follows:

1. Watch what everyone else is doing.

2. Learn from these people and note what works and what doesn't.

3. Do something slightly different.

Often, a simple way to attain speedy success in any field is to absorb the habits, traits or output of the top performers in that field, and then just *change them slightly*. Here's how:

BREAK SUCCESS DOWN INTO ITS COMPONENT PARTS

When you're examining any successful person or company, it's enormously helpful to look for 'systems' and 'patterns'.

Everything can be boiled down to a set of simple steps.

A friend of mine decided to study the 'Harry Potter' books to see if she could find why they were so gripping and successful. She began by writing down all the 'structural' details she found inside: when a plot point happened, when a new character was introduced, when the twists occurred. Slowly, she got to understand the rhythms and systems in the books and eventually concluded that (even though the 'Harry Potter' books are, of course, brilliantly written) like any success, they follow a clever, but discernible, pattern – and one that can be both learned from and also mimicked.

IT'S ALL ABOUT DECONSTRUCTION

When you figure out the pattern or system behind something, then something that looks complex will suddenly seem wonderfully simple. Once you know the 'secrets' behind a business, idea or person, you can then plan your own success using the methods you've uncovered.

And once you've worked out some of the elements to someone else's success, you then need to ensure that you use those insights to create something new. You may have the heard the powerful saying:

'DIFFERENTIATE OR DIE'

Burn this into your memory and use it always. In order to achieve any success, you must do two things:

1. GET NOTICED

2. OFFER SOMETHING DIFFERENT

Rather than 'business as usual', it's vital to strive for 'business as *unusual*'.

When I applied for my first job at the most exciting T.V. company in the U.K., I found out that more than two thousand people were going for the same position. That was quite a daunting realisation and I could easily have given in to my internal demons who were screaming at me: *'How are you any different to those other people'* and *'I'm sure there'll be better candidates than you who apply'*. The fact is, the demons may have had a point – they often do – but our demons must always be firmly pushed aside. I took a huge deep breath and bluffed onwards, and aimed to follow the methods I've outlined above in order to get noticed by offering something different.

I started by asking myself a simple question:

'WHAT IS EVERYONE ELSE DOING IN THIS SITUATION?'

The answer: everyone else was submitting their résumés and an application form for the job, exactly as the T.V. company had asked them to. Then I took the important step forward:

IN ORDER TO BE NOTICED,
ONCE YOU KNOW WHAT EVERYONE ELSE IS DOING, YOU *HAVE* TO DO SOMETHING DIFFERENT

So, as well as sending in my résumé and application form, I researched the boss of the company in such detail that I found out he adored a specific actor on a popular soap opera. I then wrote to that actor, asked them to send me a signed photo and when they did, I sent it to the boss of the company with a speech bubble that I'd stuck on, to look like it was coming from the actor's mouth, saying *'Hire Shed!'* Then after I'd managed to get through the first round of interviews for the job, one lunchtime soon afterwards, I arranged for a pizza to be delivered to the same boss, complete with a 'ransom note' style message stuck to the underside of the pizza box. It said *Wanted To Give You A Pizza My Mind...And Say Thanks For The Interview...Shed'*.

As well as stunts like this, I also sent in scripts for programme concepts and ideas for new T.V. shows. I did this because...

STUNTS ARE A GREAT WAY TO GET NOTICED, BUT ONCE YOU HAVE SOMEONE'S ATTENTION, YOU *MUST* BACK UP YOUR STUNTS WITH SOLID 'CONTENT' THAT COULD BENEFIT THE PERSON YOUR STUNT IS AIMED AT

In the end, after more interviews, I got the job at the T.V. company and stayed for six years.

As well as aiming to *differentiate* when you're trying to be successful, it's also very useful to think about the word 'remarkable'. Now, in order for you to be 'remarkable', the crucial point is that people have to *remark on you*, or *what you're doing*. In order to be remarked upon – and talked about – you have to do something to get noticed. And you'll seldom get noticed if you do what everyone else is doing. It's worth emphasising this point:

IN ORDER TO BE REMARKABLE, YOU MUST GET PEOPLE TO *REMARK* ON WHAT YOU'RE DOING

And one way you can get people to notice what you're doing is by concentrating on DETAILS.

The wonderful fact is that…

PEOPLE NOTICE LITTLE THINGS

And they both appreciate and 'bond' to them.

For example, I noticed that most books have their titles printed on the spine horizontally, so that the person looking at the book can read the title on the spine when the book is lying flat on its side. This is because most titles are too long to print vertically and also because often books are sold stacked on their sides in bookstores. However, my father pointed out to me that, actually, when you place a book on a bookshelf next to other books, it's usually placed upright – and thus if you want to find a book, you have to mentally cock your head to one side in order to read the title. Try it:

E
P
I
P
H
A
N
Y

Once this was pointed out to me, I couldn't stop noticing how my dad was right and how book spines are printed the 'wrong' way for storing in a bookcase. That's why, for the physical copy of this book, we've printed the title vertically on the spine - so you can read it downwards. And hopefully it'll stand out in the bookstore because of that difference. Hardly world-shatteringly massive, but a small detail that a) might make the book that tiny bit more remarkable and b) show I care about you, and the experience you have with something I create – and thus perhaps go towards you having a good feeling about what I do. Consequently, hopefully you'll look forward to my next creation or recommend what I do to others.

And actually, details are often the key to success and failure, because all the tiny decisions you make add up to whether people will like what you produce or do.

As a creator, you're a complete ONE-OFF...

Here's a wonderfully empowering thought:

> **IF YOU BROUGHT AN IDEA TO LIFE**
> **AND A HUNDRED RANDOM PEOPLE**
> **ALSO BROUGHT THAT IDEA TO LIFE...**
> **EACH FINISHED VERSION OF THE IDEA**
> **WOULD BE DIFFERENT AND UNIQUE**

This means that whenever you do something, only *you* will bring an idea to life in exactly the way you'll do it. That's rather comforting and gives you some protection in the long term because no one can duplicate all your decisions and thought processes exactly. Even when an idea of yours hits the real world, it's virtually impossible for someone to duplicate the way you brought the idea to the world's attention and equally impossible for them to predict how you'll bring your next creation to life – or even, what it'll be. Plus, if you're working with someone else (as I often do) the choice you make in picking who to partner with, how you work with them and the vision you set out at the start always combine to produce a strategy that's uniquely yours.

It's the multitude of tiny decisions you make in your life that produce outcomes that are only *yours*. Because no one else has had exactly the same past as you, your end 'products' and 'actions' will ALWAYS be personal to you.

And it's these tiny decisions that you make along the way that make the difference between your idea being a success or a failure.

Sometimes, it's hard to know when to stop adding details or fussing over something you do, and often there's a finite amount of time to do something, so you have to get your ideas out the best way you can in the time you have. That's fine, just be aware that each time you make a decision along the way, it'll effect how your end user will engage with what you're doing – both now and in the future. For the same reason, it's also a good idea to look for problems before they arise, as this often creates decisions that will make you stand out. So...

RATHER THEN BEING A PERFECTIONIST
BE A PRE-FECTIONIST

When you're about to send something out into the world, it's always best to try to predict the ways it could go wrong, and put it right beforehand. And wonderfully, if you plan right from the start to avoid things going wrong, this often forces you to make decisions that help you succeed.

Also, whenever you find yourself facing a setback in anything you do, it's important to remember that how you deal with that challenge will not only determine your success, it will also show yourself and those around you what kind of person you are.

When the going is good, *everyone* looks good. It's when the going gets much tougher that someone's inner strength and personality is exposed. When problems occur, the situation will immediately reveal who gets angry, who gives up, who comes up with creative solutions and who triumphs. Each hurdle is really a test to show yourself and others around you that you'll be one of the people who can triumph.

IT'S EASY TO DEAL WITH SUCCESS... IT'S HOW YOU DEAL WITH *PROBLEMS* OR *CHALLENGES* THAT REALLY SHOWS WHAT SORT OF PERSON YOU ARE... TO YOURSELF AND TO OTHERS

It's vital to be aware of this because when you hit a snag, it'll hopefully help you to pause, view it as a test, step back, take a deep breath and think of a solution to power onwards towards making your idea come alive.

'BUT SHED, I MIGHT BE COPIED!'

Once you've come up with a great idea and decided how you're going to make it happen, it's common to get a pang of worry about other people copying you and stealing your thunder.

I often get asked, *'Shed, should I spend money on protecting my idea?'* And I always answer, *'Now, if you suddenly come up with the way to create something that will categorically and fundamentally CHANGE THE WORLD, then yes, you should consider spending your time and budget on trying to protect the idea.'* Notice, I said 'trying to protect the idea', because often it's very easy for someone to tweak an idea slightly and then make another version of it. But if tomorrow you crack a way to make a car engine run on water, then you should possibly spend some money on protecting that idea, because this will be something that'll alter the car industry (and human development) forever – and you should most certainly be the one to reap the rewards of your genius!

However, most new ideas are simply variations of old ideas and, actually, what people sometimes view as a 'new idea' is often an existing idea that's been executed way better. And that's because of the decisions the person behind it made every step of the way during its development. So when you start to do something, rather than spend a lot of your effort or money on patenting, trademarking or copyrighting, it's frequently better to concentrate on creating and distributing your idea so that people will remark on it and fully engage with it, too. And one method to give you the best chance of success is to launch your concept in three ways:

BETTER, QUICKER AND LOUDER

If you can pour all your time and energy into ensuring that you follow these three guidelines, then you'll have a great chance at succeeding in everything you do.

First, what you do has to be BETTER. By 'better', I really mean 'different', in that you must offer people something (even by a small amount) they've not encountered before.

Second, it's often good to be QUICKER than others and get your idea out there AT THE RIGHT TIME, before someone else, because if you follow someone else, then your idea might not be as remarkable. The fantastic news is that as long as you carry out the 'BETTER guideline', even if you bring your idea out *after* someone else, as longs as your finished product improves on theirs in some way, and you launch with cleverer timing, you can still get a competitive edge. So, QUICKER in this instance doesn't have to mean *first*, it can simply mean *better timed*. Sometimes an idea can be launched at a certain time and flop, and the exact same idea can be launched at another time and blow big. So, it's definitely worth considering the best time to take action.

Last, when you *do* something, it's good to do it in a LOUD way, and make sure you shout about it from the rooftops. And actually, to plan exactly *how* you'll shout about it. I've launched many ideas that I believed were good, but simply because I didn't 'get them out there' into the world 'loudly' enough, they didn't connect with people – mainly because no one knew about them!

IF YOU HAVE THE BEST IDEA IN THE WORLD, IT WON'T SUCCEED UNLESS PEOPLE KNOW ABOUT IT

Sometimes we all need to remind ourselves of this, because it's SO easy to get wrapped up in your brilliant idea and how well you've made it that you naturally think *'What I've done is AMAZING and will definitely be HUGE when I launch it – people will just DISCOVER it…'*

However, because humans today are bombarded with so much information in their daily lives, you have to break though all that noise – so they can at least decide whether what you've done is fantastic or not. So, it's vital that you plan how you're going to let people know about your idea, and then tell as many as you possibly can. There are fast, clever and cheap ways of doing this, and my secrets for GETTING YOUR IDEAS OUT THERE are coming up soon.

So, the mix of BETTER, QUICKER (or CAREFULLY TIMED) and LOUDER is a killer combination that'll hopefully always get the fabulous results you're looking for.

And by the way, if you *do* crack the secret to the 'water engine', please get in touch, (simply message me through ShedSimove.com or send me a pigeon with a note on its leg). I'll be happy to help you launch the water engine and battle the evil oil cartels with you, too. That's really good of me, isn't it!

SECRET 7
TWO NEAT TRICKS FOR MOTIVATING YOURSELF

There is one undeniable fact that affects all of us, which is…

WE ARE ALL GOING TO DIE!

That's cheery isn't it!

Yes, all of us will eventually shuffle off this mortal coil.

Some sooner, some later.

REALLY SORRY TO BREAK IT YOU,
BUT YOU ARE
DEFINITELY…
ABSOLUTELY…
MOST CERTAINLY…
GOING TO DIE

Therefore, once you've digested this hard truth, you'll soon realise that…

THERE IS NO TIME LIKE THE PRESENT

It sounds like a cliché to say we have to squeeze every drop from every day – and, of course, in practice it's very hard to when you have to deal with the practicalities of life (unless your personal assistant, butler, cleaner and driver are on hand to help) but it's completely and utterly true.

THERE ARE ALWAYS REASONS WHY IT'S NOT A GOOD TIME TO START SOMETHING NEW

Some of these reasons for stopping won't even come from you.

NEWSFLASH

THERE IS NO YESTERDAY – IT'S GONE… TOMORROW IS NOT GUARANTEED… *THERE IS ONLY TODAY*

There's only today!

SO START…NOW!

Here's the second psychological trick you can use if you're ever feeling anything less than hugely confident:

I MAY NOT BELIEVE I'M TALENTED *NOW*… BUT I AM GOING TO PUSH AND LEARN UNTIL I AM

It's a very common feeling to worry that you're not up to a certain job or to doubt yourself. The way I encourage myself to carry on is to think about this fact: *'I'll only ever have the chance at being good at something if I start trying to do it.'* Seems kind of obvious, I know. But, actually, sometimes it's very daunting trying something you've never done before because you frequently think about how much you don't know about conquering the task ahead. And this can stop you from starting! The way around this roadblock is to 'trick' yourself into believing that the first day you actually start making your idea come to life will be the last day you'll be a total novice in that area. As soon as you decide to begin, you can immediately look forward to having more expertise than you do now.

ACTUALLY, IT'S NOT REALLY A TRICK, IT'S A FACT

The moment you start something new, you instantly become more experienced in that field. If you don't ever start a new idea then, by definition, you'll always be inexperienced at doing that task. The only way to break the cycle of letting 'lack of knowledge' stop you from starting something new is to plunge in with the certainty that you'll soon NOT be inexperienced!

This kind of thinking helps take the pressure off you, because it means you're less likely to avoid starting something because you don't think you're good enough, or beat yourself up if you make a mistake. The fact is, your great brain is designed to *learn*, so just plough on with your journey, do your best, make adjustments when they're needed and remember that you're getting more experienced every day you continue with your goal.

SECRET 8
HOW TO GET RICH (FAIRLY) QUICK

And now, for your ultimate pleasure and bank balance, I'm going to tell you how to become fabulously wealthy.

Wow, this book is well worth the cover price isn't it!

Success comes in many forms, but often in our capitalist society, success is seen in terms of 'money'. Well, I say that's not the whole story. In my opinion, being 'healthy' is the only true measure of success because when you're well and your brain is functioning, you can accomplish anything. It's no good having millions in the bank if you're dying of an incurable disease or you're hit by a bus.

However, being rich can certainly alleviate some of life's worries and allow you to choose what you want to do every day (isn't that what we all want, after all?). And there are certainly upsides to having money. We all know that *'Money can't buy happiness'*, but I figure that, if you're going to be depressed at some points in your life (and we all will be), at least money can allow you to be depressed in your mansion, surrounded by masseuses and Champagne.

But, bear in mind that when it comes down to it, all that really matters in life is whether you can 'do' or 'communicate' – and that's what I mean by being 'healthy'. People with massive paralysis in their bodies, and even only the ability to blink, have achieved huge successes and written influential books, so if they can achieve success, you and I certainly can too.

Anyway, if you still want to be rich, there are two main secrets that may help you focus your endeavours:

FIND OUT WHAT TURNS YOU ON
FOLLOW A PASSION

Of course, there are lots of ways to become rich, but doing what you love is the easiest and most enjoyable way to earn wads of cash.

It's also the prudent way.

Your passion for a certain area of life will drive you to overcome challenges and seek solutions – and they are two of the keys to success. So you simply need to find something that EXCITES you.

So how do you do this?

Question: What person do you look at and say, *'I wish I could get paid for what they do.'*

Also dig deep. What things do you think about a lot every day?

You might find that you think a lot about something not usually directly related to business or work – for example family, travel or even sex *(well, it's natural!)* and you might not immediately think about a 'career' working in these areas. But, if a certain area of interest really gets you fired up when you think about it, then there will always be a business related to this sector – and if there isn't, you can set up your own!

There are businesses built around virtually every human activity. So, what all of us must do is find out which activity we love being part of, and then gravitate to any businesses that deal with them…

Once you've got a vague idea of the direction you want your life to go in, you can always dip your toe in the water and try working in a certain sector to see if it actually does rock your world.

FOCUS IS VITAL

Try to gravitate to a life that will really hold your attention, because then you won't be distracted – and when you focus on something for a while, you not only get things done, you naturally get better at it.

Another question: If you won the lottery, after buying some new things and doing some travel, what would you actually want to do each day?

THERE'S YOUR GOAL

SECRET 9
SECRET 009: LICENCE TO EARN

There's a slightly shocking, but eye-opening phrase that some people use to describe anyone who is employed in a traditional job:

'WAGE SLAVE'

This might seem rather harsh on the face of it, but there's a large nugget of truth here: people who are employed by others and have a 'conventional job' can be described as 'wage slaves' because they're in a situation that only pays them when they're actually *working*. They're therefore tied to attending their job in order to earn a wage. If they don't work, they get no money. Pretty much everyone has done this at some point and I certainly have, too.

This might seem like a reasonable way to generate your income, but it's not the very best way to use your time – because it means that you only earn money when you're physically present at work.

In the past, while working my socks off for a company, it always slightly jarred with me that all of us fellow workers were actually building a company (and often pieces of sellable content too) that the person (or people) who owned that company could sell at a later date.

Now, you might say...

'THIS IS WESTERN CAPITALISM, MY FRIEND!'

The fundamental gap between what a worker produces and what they're paid is what allows the boss to make profit. Some people might even say that workers are exploited. In any case, the fact remains that a boss running a company uses the workers to create long-term potential wealth and income. This is because the company can be sold off at a later date and any creations that the workers make are owned by the company and can then be sold over and over in the future, bringing the owners more income – crucially, for no more work. The workers, on the other hand, get short-term income because when they stop work, they stop getting paid.

The 'wage slave' concept deeply affected me as soon as I heard it, and from that moment, this influential notion burned fiercely in my mind. The 'burning' made me yearn to find out how I could earn a living where I was able to choose what I wanted to do every day and also own a stake in anything I created or worked on. It took a while for me to actually discover the exact method of working that gave me all of this, and I hope that process I went through might also help you focus on what could make you successful and happy as well.

When I first started creating gift products and was forced to get many of my products made by myself – by finding factories in China, shipping products over and then searching for people who would sell my stuff, I quickly noticed that I enjoyed some parts of this process very much more than others.

I realised that I adored the creative side of bringing something to life and, specifically, that I loved coming up with the products, shaping the development of the item, getting it right and then marketing the finished article. On the flip side, I had much less fondness for (and consequently wasn't very good at) the logistical or administrative tasks I encountered – the shipping, warehousing, invoicing and distribution. But unfortunately, all parts of the process are vitally important, and none can be ignored.

So, I began to look around for models of working that would allow me to focus on what I loved, while giving me some ownership in what I was working on all day. I decided that I needed to find experts to partner with who were much better than me at certain parts of the process. By doing this, my ultimate 'pure income' would most likely be lower, but I'd be doing much more of what I wanted to do, every single day. For me, the decision was easy.

My main motivation in life back then (and still now, actually) wasn't particularly to be 'wealthy'. We all need a certain level of income to survive, of course, but for me, my big aim was – and still is – to have a healthy, stimulating, fun, unique and creatively fulfilling day, every day of my life. Some people (most likely, wealthy billionaires) might say this is a cop-out, but actually, it's a very clear lifestyle choice. I forced myself to focus hard on exactly what activities I really wanted to do in the day, and sorting out shipping schedules just wasn't one of them. So, I decided that if someone else took care of all the things I wasn't good at and allowed me to be free to do things that did indeed enrich my soul, this was worth far more to me than a bit more cash in the bank.

What's more, I also believe that if you do what you *totally love* for long enough, you'll get financially rich anyway. It may take a bit longer, but the journey (and your stories) will be better. So, it's most definitely best to focus on what you adore – and work in that area.

For me, when every day is different, I'm meeting amazing people and going to incredible places, then I feel hugely successful. But of course, many people, and Western society as a whole, measures 'wealth' as success. Luckily, I was able to find a solution that gave me a bit of both.

LICENSING YOUR IDEAS CAN FREE YOU UP TO THINK OF MORE IDEAS

Ideally, if you can, you should always be looking to invest your precious time (and money, if you're lucky enough to have any spare) in something that will continue to grow in value after you have stopped working on it the first time, or has the potential to be sold for a higher price in the future.

The way to do this is to own something, have a share in it – or to license your creations out. As you know, licensing involves you allowing a partner company to use or develop something of yours and then the company pays you a regular fee to do so, often a percentage of the profit that the idea brings.

POSSESSION IS NINE-TENTHS OF THE LAW AND IT'S QUITE A FEW TENTHS OF BEING SUCCESSFUL, TOO

Examples of activities that make money while you sleep…

You could negotiate a profit share, run a company, own stocks and shares, buy property or land, create a product – or license an idea…or even write a book about how to make anything you desire come to life…

SECRET 10
FAILING UPWARDS
(OR PLEASE, PLEASE FAIL)

FAILING IS SOMETHING TO STRIVE FOR
YOU MUST LEARN TO *WANT* TO FAIL

Conventional wisdom says that mistakes are 'bad' and should be avoided at all costs. Well, that stops now. Because both you and I should throw open the windows and proclaim:

'MISTAKES ARE GREAT!'

I'd like to try and plant a seed in your mind so that you'll begin to actively chase the process of making mistakes, because only then will you know you're on the road to success.

Of course, if you're a heart surgeon, this wisdom has a slightly different resonance – I'm not advocating you aim to make lots of mistakes in your day-to-day work (we don't want anyone to die now, do we...) – but the principle still stands. Even the pioneers of heart surgery tried new procedures on animal hearts (and even some live, human hearts) before they got it exactly right. The important fact to remember is that no progress is made unless new ideas are tried.... *and mistakes are made.*

You must trick your mind to look forward to mistakes, so when one happens, you can say:

'COOL, I MADE A MISTAKE –
THAT MEANS I'VE JUST LEARNED
ONE MORE LESSON THAT WILL TAKE ME
CLOSER TO MY GOAL'

Keep this in mind:

IF YOU'RE MAKING MISTAKES,
YOU'RE BEING SUCCESSFUL

A mistake or 'failure' is simply a wonderful sign that you're trying something new. Also, mistakes usually throw up surprising opportunities and are rarely ever dead ends. They either spur you on to a better strategy or something comes from the mistake that you didn't expect, plus they can often lead you to an interesting discovery or adventure anyway. A 'failure' isn't necessarily always a 'failure' – sometimes the failure is actually a success in a different form than you planned.

When I was thirty, I filmed a documentary that caused a big scandal in the press – it was never actually aired and ruined my career for a bit (not quite the outcome I was hoping for!). Some people viewed this as a catastrophic failure and, at the time, I felt that as well…But actually, the whole episode taught me a powerful lesson about 'lying' and also gave me the skills to achieve many other tasks in my life after that. I'll be letting you know more about that story, very soon…

There are countless examples of how 'mistakes' have led to enormously positive outcomes and discoveries. You might have heard how Post-it Notes were invented when the geniuses at 3M attempted to create a very strong glue and 'failed' to do so, instead making a weak glue, which they then discovered was perfect for sticking up and re-sticking little paper memos. In fact, many 'leaps forward' came from 'mistakes' including the discovery of penicillin, holes in doughnuts, Silly Putty and even cheese.

Another superb example of a 'mistake' having a positive outcome is when a pricing error caused the U.S. fashion website Zappos to lose over $1.5 million. After the mistake was discovered, the bosses took the decision to honour the low prices, resulting in enormous positive publicity, a surge of new customers and a mammoth rise in goodwill and loyalty for the brand; an outcome that money simply can't buy.

What all these examples show is that first, you MUST be *trying* something or *doing* something in order for any outcome to happen at all. And then, when you do start to make something happen or try something new, sometimes the results will be as you expect (or even, hope), but sometimes they won't be – and these results are often misnamed 'failures' or 'mistakes'. Importantly, neither of these outcomes is necessarily automatically 'good' or 'bad'. Unexpected results might feel like catastrophes at the time but, actually, they can often lead to something entirely unexpected, exciting and positive. Often, 'successful' and happy people will tell you've they've made many mistakes over their life. Well, I'm here to go one further:

I FAIL EVERY SINGLE DAY

Like many people who like to make things happen (and who others sometimes call 'successful'), I have made, and continue to make, tons and tons of mistakes – and indeed, I continue to 'fail' on a regular basis. It's not that I'm utterly stupid and don't learn from the mistakes I've made, it's just that when you're constantly pushing yourself and trying new things, you never know all the answers, so mistakes are simply part of the territory.

Of course, like you, I don't actually *like* making mistakes, and actively take steps to avoid doing so. It's highly frustrating and tiring not getting something right or reaching your goals right away. But I've learned to relax much more in my approach to 'failure' because now I know that mistakes and setbacks are simply signifiers to me that I'm trying hard to reach a new goal. This brings me comfort because it shows I'm not standing still and also (if I learn from my mistakes, which I always try to do) experiencing mistakes shows me that I'm definitely getting better in my ability to conquer the new area I've decided to pursue.

Now then, at this point, here's a very cheesy perspective for you, but you might just remember it because it's so cringe-worthy (I hope you'll forgive me):

IT'S CALLED A 'MISTAKE' BECAUSE YOU ALWAYS 'TAKE' SOMETHING FROM IT

Ta da! You can stop groaning now.

Here's another trick to play on yourself that may just make your journey to success a bit more fun and way less daunting:

DON'T BE THE BEST... BE THE WORST!

If you decided to play a game with yourself and aim for 'total failure' in any particular area by doing something new, but really badly on purpose, you'll very probably find out how close you really are to huge success and also whether that whole area actually fires your imagination, too.

Kidding yourself that you'll try to be the worst at some new task you're trying to tackle also takes some of the pressure off you because, in effect, you're then 'playing' at trying something. You put less stress on yourself to be totally amazing right away and thus remove some of the apprehension about starting, because the bar is set so low in your mind. If you aim to be bad at something and then you are, you'll chuckle to yourself at being bad, but very often you'll also see that with a few tweaks, you could – if you wanted to – be very good at doing something in the new area you're playing in.

WE ALL 'FEEL THE FEAR'

As well as 'internally pretending' to deliberately set out to be 'bad' at carrying out a particular new task, you can also minimise any fears you might have of 'failing' by telling yourself that you're going to set your targets of performance very, very low. Then, when you see how easy it is to reach those low targets – and what you've learned along the way – you'll naturally set more goals knowing that you can tackle the same task again to an even higher standard.

SECRET 11
THE ONLY THING MEN DO BETTER THAN WOMEN

There's a fine art that's very helpful for success and it's something men seem to do more than women. And that's probably because it's a slightly vulgar behaviour! The particular trait I'm talking about is…

THE FINE ART OF SELF-PROMOTION

In order to succeed in whatever you want to do, it's often vital that you sell yourself and maximise the potential you have, not only so that people can be aware of what you're doing (and either engage with it or pay for it), but also so that you can persuade others who can help you on your path to success to team up with you.

Because all adults are essentially bluffing their way through life and business, with a little bit of preparation and some fake confidence, you can too. So, it's useful to learn how to push yourself forwards as a 'commodity' or 'product'.

Now, just to be clear, when I talk about *self-promotion* or *pushing yourself forward*, I'm most certainly not advocating *lying*. Absolutely, not – lying should be avoided at all costs, because it causes people to lose trust in you and once you've lost that, people can't have a relationship with you. And the relationships you forge are one of the keys to success.

What I *am* saying though, is that...

IT'S GOOD TO 'BIG YOURSELF UP'

In fact, a lot of success is about how you perceive yourself and the situation you're in, because that sets up whether you'll have enough energy to begin something. Curiously, there's rarely one true *reality* because we each have our own. This is why you and I might see a situation in one way, and someone else might view it in a completely different way. Even though we may think we're right and they're wrong, there's no actual 'right' really. Curiously, this effect can be seen all around us. A lot of men (mostly) exhibit a fascinating disparity in how they see themselves and how talented they actually are (or at least, how talented *I believe* some of them are!). I call this...

THE CONFIDENCE DELUSION

We all know people who seem to be supremely confident in what they do or say. And sometimes, there are people who display an enormous confidence that doesn't perhaps match up to their ability. Now, confidence has *enormous* power. When someone supremely confident encounters other people, it makes those people believe what that person says. And, ultimately, when humans in a group *believe* something, they can make anything happen. So, watch how people with 'the confidence delusion' work, learn from their swagger and try to delude yourself a little too. Aim hard to laser in on your good points, remind yourself of them and believe in your uniqueness. Once you believe, others will too – and they'll want to help you achieve your goals.

EVERYONE HAS MASSIVE SKILL GAPS

When I decided I wanted to become a product designer, I had no training, no knowledge of the retail industry and actually couldn't even draw very well. But with the help of free images and graphics found on the internet, some sticky tape and card, I created visualisations and prototypes that started to bring my ideas to life. I then went to trade fairs – and announced myself as a 'product designer'. I wasn't actually a *qualified* 'product designer', but in a way I was still indeed a 'product designer' because I'd come up with new ideas that had potential to become original items.

And now, of course, after successfully launching many products into the global market, albeit with the help of many experts in the field, people view me as a successful product designer. But I still can't draw and still have to get brilliantly skilled graphic designers to help me with my designs. It just shows you that you can always fill in any skill gaps you have, simply by working with people who have those skills. And moreover, that when it comes to 'doing anything' *there's always a way*, especially if you…

TUNE INTO YOUR INNER CHUTZPAH

'Self-promotion' is an important talent to cultivate. It allowed me to view myself as a product designer even when I wasn't officially trained, and then, because I acted like a real product designer, I eventually came to be viewed as one.

This art of self-promotion, of 'walking the walk' and 'talking the talk', is the only thing (mostly) men do much better than women. Women are way more talented in pretty much all other areas, but in the area of self-promotion, there's room for improvement.

Chutzpah is a slang word for 'guts', 'cheek' or 'balls'. When someone asks questions that no one else asks or puts themselves in situations that most people might shy away from, they are said to have massive 'chutzpah'.

Not all of us naturally have this trait. So, it's good to play a trick on your mind by imagining yourself as someone else. Imagine you have no fear, no barriers and no worries about doing anything. See yourself in your mind's eye as a superhero, standing on top of a mountain with your cape billowing. YOU ARE NOW *'CHUTZPAH MAN'* or

'CHUTZPAH WOMAN'. Next time you're in a situation that demands you take action quickly, imagine yourself as this superhero and ask yourself:

'WHAT WOULD CHUTZPAH MAN OR CHUTZPAH WOMAN DO?'

That's right – they'd charge on in confidently and get the job done.

SELF PROMOTION SHOULDN'T BE ABOUT 'ARROGANCE'

IT'S ABOUT FOCUSING ON WHAT YOU DO WELL AND THEN COMMUNICATING TO OTHERS THAT YOU HAVE THESE SKILLS – AND USING THEM WITH 150% CONVICTION

I'm not advocating rudeness either, I'm just reminding you how important it is to politely push as far as you can go in any situation – you'll be amazed what happens if you ask for the Earth.

IF YOU SHOOT FOR THE STARS, YOU'LL REACH THE MOON...

GO FOR THE IMPOSSIBLE... AND SOMETIMES YOU REACH IT

THEN, WONDERFULLY, PEOPLE WON'T TELL YOU THAT WHAT YOU'VE DONE IS *'IMPOSSIBLE'* ANY MORE...

SECRET 12
'NEGNETS' AND HOW TO AVOID THEM

When you're trying to make your goals happen, there are enough obstacles in your way to make it extremely hard to carry on. And the effect that other people around you can have, is also absolutely pivotal.

THERE ARE PEOPLE YOU SHOULD AVOID
AT THE START OF CREATING SOMETHING NEW...

I CALL THEM 'NEGNETS'

There are certain people who are like magnets for negative energy, hence 'negative magnets' or 'Negnets' for short. These are the people who seem to both collect and also emanate negative energy. They have an incredible (and damaging) knack of passing this negative energy on to others, including you – and it's powerfully sticky. Negative energy can severely hamper your progress, or sometimes even stop you from reaching your goal. A Negnet is the sort of person who might say *'That's an awful idea'* or *'That'll never work.'*

The fact of the matter remains that...

THERE ARE ALWAYS
MANY, MANY REASONS
OTHER PEOPLE CAN FIND
FOR WHY AN IDEA WON'T WORK

Before you decide to begin making one of your ideas happen, it's so easy to find dozens of reasons why it may not work. You may well have these doubts yourself. Your inner demons will be hugely happy to offer you many reasons why you might not succeed, and numerous other people will be more than happy to find them for you, too. What's much more difficult is having a positive vision, making sure you're always searching for ways to move forward and overcome obstacles – and to stay sharply focused on the goal ahead, so you can make your idea happen.

Sometimes, someone can instantly take the wind from your sails with just a slight movement of their face that registers disapproval of your idea. Or they can say it aloud to your face. Both are equally harmful to any goal you want to achieve, and you must be very aware of this negativity occurring, so you can guard against its destructive force and then quickly dismiss it.

So, it's definitely best to avoid telling any Negnets your ideas at the start and it's a VERY good plan to...

TELL NO ONE ABOUT YOUR IDEA UNTIL

YOU'VE BROUGHT IT TO LIFE IN SOME WAY

That way, you'll protect your child (idea) until it's ready to at least have a go at fending for itself.

So, when you're trying to get an idea off the ground, identify any Negnets in your life, and no matter how close you are to them, try to avoid talking to these Negnets about your ideas or goals, and especially right at the beginning when the idea is just a concept in your head. At this point, your idea is way, way too fragile and you can't risk it being shattered by some flippant remark, disapproving look or discouraging comment.

The next secret will outline how you can make any idea you have much, much stronger, so it'll gain valuable protection from the Negnets who you're bound to meet along the way to success.

SECRET 13
BE LIKE FRANKENSTEIN

As I'm sure you know, the fictional character 'Frankenstein' was actually the doctor who created the monster and not the monster itself.

Frankenstein gave life to a collection of dead body parts that, with a dramatic burst of electricity, created a new person. And, in the same way, it's absolutely essential that you give life to every idea you have. Each idea you think up is like a delicate newborn baby. And unless you give it two things, it can easily die. You must be extremely careful not to lose your ideas, because often when an idea goes away, it rarely returns…

Your idea is a like a delicate infant.

It needs nurturing and protecting.

It needs:

FOOD

ARMOUR

The food part is easy. The way you give it food is to think about it and develop it – and to do this, the first step is to remember your great idea.

You need to give every single idea you come up with some **FOOD** RIGHT WAY – and the most important meal you can give your idea is to…

WRITE IT DOWN OR MAKE A NOTE OF IT

This is vital to ensure your idea doesn't instantly die. How often have you thought of a fantastic idea, only to forget it a few hours later or the next day? We've all done it. And those ideas hardly ever return.

So, it's vital that you record your idea IMMEDIATELY. Write it down on a piece of paper, chisel it in stone or paint it on a nearby cow. Do whatever you can to ensure that you'll remember it later.

Sometimes, when an idea pops into my head and I don't have a pen handy, I phone my answering machine at home and leave myself a message about the idea I've just thought up that second. Then, when I return home, I listen to my message and make a proper note of the idea in a notebook or on my computer.

People sometimes don't give much value to an idea in someone's head, and yet…

ALL HUMAN ACHIEVEMENT HAS COME FROM AN IDEA IN SOMEONE'S HEAD

But, unless an idea of yours is firmly recorded and remembered, there's nothing to build on, no starting point for an adventure or chance to make some money, no nugget of genius, *nothing* that can develop. And yet, without your actions that follow, there will also be nothing. But the difference between the 'idea' and 'action' in this case, is that you, or indeed other people, can always provide the 'action' at a later date. Whereas your initial 'idea' is often dreamed up only once, solely by you, and if it isn't nourished right away it dies there and then. Once an idea of yours is stored in some concrete way, it will ALWAYS have the potential to flourish – and enhance your life. It could still be a 'seed' waiting to grow for years…

So, it's absolutely crucial you get into the habit of recording your ideas.

Now, once you've saved your idea somewhere safe, you also need to give it some **ARMOUR.**

Even when you've recorded your idea and have the opportunity to easily recall it, it's still highly vulnerable. The risk now changes from the idea not even being 'born', to the risk of it being killed by others – or even in some cases, by you.

One great way to protect your idea is to breathe some more life into by creating a…

PROTOTYPE or VISUALISATION

When an idea is a line of words on a piece of paper or computer screen, it has a small amount of power. Indeed, anything you do that gets the idea from being just 'words you speak', or a 'thought in your head', is a huge leap forward. Words on paper or a screen at least give your idea a chance of life and make your idea way, way more robust than words in your head. But to give an idea even more force – and protect it during its journey ahead, you must turn those words into some kind of initial mock-up, rough sketch or model. This will immediately give your idea a massive boost in power.

So, every time you come up with an idea, whether you think it's totally great or even just 'okay', you must record it straight away. Then later, you can go back through your ideas, pick and choose the ones that excite you – and decide which one (or more) to bring to life by creating a mock-up, visualisation or prototype. That way, you'll ensure that your ideas have the very best chance of coming to life and giving you the success you deserve.

SECRET 14
AVOIDING THESE THREE EMOTIONS WILL HELP YOU

During your journey towards success, it's completely natural to go through a wide range of emotional states. You'll have setbacks that are frustrating, and lots of wins that are invigorating and soul-enriching. When you go through this range of emotions, this signifies to you that you're LIVING LIFE to the full and making the most of your valuable time on the planet by making things happen that excite and delight you.

Some emotions that you might naturally experience along the way might not be so beneficial though, and it's a good idea to keep an eye out for these and to realise the possible effects they can have.

These emotions are…

RUDENESS

ANGER

JEALOUSY

Try not to be rude...

This one is easier said than done. However, it's an important secret to bear in mind, especially when things get tough (because they will). If you can pull this one off, even some of the time, you'll always be glad you did.

There's a proverb that I think about on the rare occasion I find myself in a situation that might provoke rudeness or anger. It goes like this:

> *'In an argument when two people are shouting at each other, it's hard to make out the FOOL. But, when one person is shouting and the other is calm, it's easy to make out the fool'.*

So, it's best not to be 'a fool' if at all possible.

YOU FIND OUT THE TRUE MEASURE OF SOMEONE WHEN THINGS ARE GOING BADLY

When difficulties rear their head, how you (and others) deal with those difficulties will starkly reveal the character of those involved. What's more…

HOW YOU DEAL WITH PROBLEMS WILL DETERMINE HOW SUCCESSFUL YOU ARE

It's good to be nice to people, and not just because being a decent human being is the only way we're going to properly evolve as humans. But, also, if you're pitching to someone in business, then there are added benefits of being a pleasure to be around.

People do business with others for two main reasons:

1. They're attracted by a great deal or a good price.

2. They like the people they're going to work with.

I'm sure you can think of an example in your own life when you've been in a situation where a certain business has offered you a better price or a more convenient service, but...*you still stay loyal to another business because you already know the people who run that business – and like them.*

NICE GUYS CAN FINISH FIRST

And so they should. Studies of reciprocity and important experiments with evolutionary models have both shown that being altruistic and kind to others is a beneficial trait for all concerned and for a functioning society. But, actually, the biggest reason to be 'nice' is simply to be a decent human and touch people's lives in a good way for the limited time that you're on the planet.

Another crucial trait you need to succeed is the ability to...

DO WHAT YOU SAY YOU'RE GOING TO DO

TRUST is hugely important. Being truthful is pretty much *everything* when it comes to both business and personal relationships. If you say you'll do something, then you must do it. In fact, it's WAY better to avoid saying you'll do something than to say you *will* do something and then not stick to your word.

Many times in your personal life, it pays to do what you've said you will, even though you might be tempted not to in the short term. Here's a very basic example. Say you decided to throw a party and immediately before the day of the event, you got the clear feeling that no one was going to turn up to your celebration. You must stick to your original plan and absolutely still throw the party. This is important for the people who do come to the party, because they'll see you're someone who does what they say (and someone who doesn't let them down after making an arrangement) and it's also crucial because the people who don't attend your party will still know that you went ahead with your plan and that'll give them huge confidence that you'll make your next party (or any other idea) happen in the future.

So, in both your personal life and in business, people need to know that you are *reliable*. This is partly because so much of life *isn't* reliable. What's more, in business life, people are very busy, so they want to work with people who are decent and do a good job, with minimum hassle to them – and a large part of 'doing a good job' is doing what you say. As soon as you let someone down you put your future in jeopardy, because then the other person will start to doubt you and your word and, at that point, might well look elsewhere. It's much better to tell someone you can't do something than say you can and then let them down later. If you do fail to deliver after categorically stating you'll do something, it won't be long until they choose to search for someone else who keeps their word. If you don't do what you say, that person is unlikely to deal with you again or recommend you to others. In fact, they'll most likely say *'Don't deal with them – they messed me around'*. No one likes to be aggravated or caused extra challenges. So it's completely crucial to be reliable, because if you aren't, you'll very likely lose a business or personal relationship.

The rule of thumb that's best to stick to is:

DON'T SAY YOU'RE GOING TO DO SOMETHING UNLESS YOU ABSOLUTELY, DEFINITELY KNOW YOU CAN AND WILL

By carefully sticking to this rule, you'll gain a reputation as a person who delivers. This is so important. It will make you grow.

I learned a hard lesson about the damaging effects of 'lying' and 'letting people down' when I filmed the T.V. documentary that I mentioned earlier. I was thirty years old at the time and here's what happened…

I set out to make a programme that would remind anyone watching about the huge value of young people and how great teachers in schools can make such a massive difference to their pupils' lives. As well as these important running themes, I also wanted to produce a show that was highly original and engaging, so I came up with an edgy way to get the programme noticed.

My big idea was this: before we began filming, we found an excellently run school that was similar to the high school I'd attended when I was growing up. We told the teachers and pupils that we were going to film them for a new T.V. show about young people and great teachers. This was true. We also told them that we wanted to film a new pupil coming into the school, who was aged sixteen. This was not so true. In fact, the sixteen-year-old boy was actually me, aged thirty, with big retainers on my teeth and my hair gelled down. Because I looked young for my age – and because the people in the school were welcoming and lovely, no one questioned my age and I spent nine weeks at the school posing as a teenage schoolboy.

It was actually the hardest thing I've ever done, lying to good people day after day – and this was to be my undoing. At the end of the filming period, we had the most amazing documentary on tape. Not only was what happened to me pretty remarkable, we also filmed the exceptional pupils and teachers in the school, plus many moving moments that showed how great teaching can change young people's lives and set them up for success. I thought that we'd have something important to say about the education system and the potential of young adults all over the world. But I was in for a shock...

At first, when I revealed my true age, the teachers and pupils were confused and then they quickly became furious. And here's the kicker: when I tried to explain why I'd made the show, I found I was sunk. Because I'd established myself as someone who had lied, they didn't believe my reasons for posing as a sixteen-year-old and the people in the school felt betrayed, humiliated and hurt. And when I look back, that's totally understandable. The show never aired and it caused both me and them a huge amount of trauma. Ever since then, I've tried VERY hard not to lie…

LYING IS DESTRUCTIVE TO PERSONAL AND BUSINESS RELATIONSHIPS

AND LETTING PEOPLE DOWN IS A FORM OF LYING

So, if you go out of your way to always do what you say, your business and personal life will thrive.

As well as sticking to your word, there's other ways of behaving that will benefit you…

DON'T BE IRRITATING, PUSHY OR ANNOYING

Every single interaction you have with another person is pivotal. You're only as good as your last meeting. You must be positive. It's fine to be keen, enthusiastic or persistent, but as soon as you are *too* pushy, irritating or rude, they might well consider going elsewhere. So, you must judge how hard you push *very* carefully.

Anyone you deal with along your journey to success will deal with many people in their day-to-day life and, potentially, could deal with many more in the future. Therefore, make sure they think about you in a positive way and all their interactions with you are positive – or they'll just cut you out.

Especially when you're planning to approach someone new for help, it's prudent to ask yourself if you're likely to be irritating or annoying or if you'll definitely help them in some way and deliver benefit.

It's always good to be polite and considerate – so, remember the little things too, like turning off your mobile phone in meetings (it's polite and shows you're focused on the person you're with) and leaving the meeting with a smile.

Anger: beware the red mist

Whatever you do, no matter how much someone annoys you in business, it's definitely best to avoid showing your anger if at all possible. You might be totally fuming inside, but you must try not to show it; it's always unattractive, powerfully negative and rarely productive.

If you can, avoid getting angry, especially in writing – because then it's an even more powerful reminder that someone can reread and instantly be reminded of how negatively you felt about them.

TRY YOUR HARDEST NOT TO MAKE
ANY DISAGREEMENTS PERSONAL

This one is tough! But it's always better to look at issues rather than blaming people or getting angry with them.

When you find yourself in a situation that makes you feel frustrated or angry, try to take a deep breath and attempt to remember a great experience you've had in the past that reminds you of how good you are with people or how you completed a task superbly well. These memories might just reset your mind to a more helpful level and put things into perspective, allowing you to deal with the situation calmly and not make yourself hard to work with.

Jealousy: the monster you can avoid

There is another feeling that we all have that's good to keep your eye on…

THE GREEN-EYED MONSTER

Being *jealous* of someone else is an emotion that we've all felt at one time or another. It's natural to compare – simply a human trait. But it's actually hugely freeing and rather wonderful to realise some 'absolute truths' about our place in the grand scheme of things. When I was starting out at work, and I began to compare myself to others, my Dad always used to say:

'Shed, you never know what's in someone's bank account...

...or how their insides are...'

That clever wisdom has stayed with me all my life. We ALL have times in our life when we are doing well, and times when things are really tough. And no matter how successful someone might appear, you never know exactly how much money they have, or way more importantly, how happy or healthy they are. *Everyone* has problems at some point in their lives, no matter how successful they may seem to be.

So, even though it's natural to compare yourself to others, try not to. Instead, make sure you're concentrating on what'll make *you* happy and healthy. It's crucial to take comfort in the fact that even people you may *think* are doing well still don't know what's round the corner for them. Plus, they'll never have your unique way of looking at things or dealing with people.

Sometimes in life it's useful to imagine a scenario that can help you be the kind of person you want to be:

**IMAGINE IF YOU FOUND YOURSELF
BEING FILMED TWENTY-FOUR HOURS A DAY
FOR A REALITY T.V. SHOW...**

Would you act any differently if you knew everybody could see what you're doing? Or if the whole world could watch how you react to situations?

There are always two sides to a story in any situation. You might feel you're totally justified at being angry, rude or jealous, but the other person involved may not – and be very surprised at how you react. In some situations, your reaction could even be a deal breaker. I've been in a few sticky scenarios where one person has got angry with another (maybe justifiably) and as they vented, they let what they said get personal and ended up attacking the other person's worth or value as a person. Big mistake. Then, the person on the receiving end of this attack never wanted to work with them again…

So, it's a great plan to try to keep an eye on the 'red mist' and other less productive emotions too. Instead of letting it ruin your relationships or distract you from your goals, try instead to channel it into making you take a deep breath and top up your energy bank, so you can stay focused on getting what you're doing very successfully accomplished.

SECRET 15
'F.O.C. IT!'

Here's a useful tool to break down a task – or indeed your whole life – so that you can ensure you'll have the best chance of success. It consists of three points:

FOCUS

OPPORTUNITIES

CHOICES

Here's the F.O.C. breakdown:

FOCUS is what you choose to spend your time and thoughts on each day. You can ask yourself: *'What do I currently think about the most?'* and if that gives you an answer about something you LIKE, it's a good idea to move towards it. If it doesn't, then you must ask yourself, *'What would I actually LOVE to do all day?'*

OPPORTUNITIES are everywhere and you must learn to recognise them. And when you're fortunate enough to be given an opportunity, you must go all out to make it count and ensure you perform to your best ability. Then, after you've performed well in that opportunity, more opportunities just like it will follow.

At this point, it's important to note that there are TWO TYPES OF OPPORTUNITIES in life:

1. 'PUSH' OPPORTUNITIES

Often when you're starting anything or shooting for a big goal, you'll be forced to create push opportunities. These are opportunities that you have to create yourself, and they can only be created through your own planning and hard work. When creating this type of opportunity, you're forced to make the first move and must 'push' the opportunity to happen. You have no option but to make an approach to someone and risk 'rejection' and 'failure', which, as you know, are both signifiers that you're on the right track to success, even though they might not feel hugely positive at the time.

When you're trying to create push opportunities, the power balance is frequently in the other person's hands because you're asking them to listen to you, consider your proposal and then decide whether they want to be part of making your goals happen.

For example, when I first decided to become a professional corporate speaker and perform presentations on innovation and creativity, I had to battle very hard to persuade people to give me a chance to speak at their company or event. I frequently got told *'No'*, or told something like *'Sorry… you're not high profile enough'* or *'experienced enough'* or *'… not quite the right type of thing we're looking for'*.

Now, knockbacks are always really hard to take, plus it's easy (and normal) to take them personally and get temporarily demoralised. But you must try to USE YOUR MENTAL ARMOUR, work a bit harder and let the knockbacks wash over you like 'water off a duck's back'. Eventually, you DEFINITELY will persuade people to help you and work with you. It just may take a bit longer than you first thought (or wanted) and require your considerable resilience. Moreover, the fact of the matter remains that unless you create these push opportunities, you'll never get the other type of opportunities, which pretty much all of us enjoy far more. And they are…

2. 'PULL' OPPORTUNITIES

A way more attractive state of affairs is when someone approaches YOU and gives you opportunities to do what you want or to be part of what they're doing, or even to enquire if you need their help with what you're doing next.

Push and pull opportunities are the difference between you 'pitching' – and you being 'pitched to'. There's something particularly fantastic when you get called up and given a pull opportunity that comes from an outside source. Not only does it mean that the person contacting you thinks what you do has value, (which is positively fulfilling in itself) it also means you're in the simply brilliant position of having an opportunity come to you, without any work or hassle whatsoever, while also having the luxury to decide whether to take it or not.

Rather than knocking on doors one after another, trying to make them open (the process of creating push opportunities), with pull opportunities you'll have doors opening in front of you and people wanting to 'pull' you through them.

After much 'pushing', I managed to create opportunities for myself to present my corporate speeches to companies, albeit often for free, at the start. After many presentations where I stumbled, delivered information unclearly or discovered areas where I could improve, I constantly honed and tweaked my performances. These improvements would never have occurred without me first pushing to make the opportunities happen, then grabbing those opportunities with both hands and wholeheartedly throwing myself into them.

And now, I'm in the marvellous 'pulling' position where people invite ME to present to their company – and pay me to do so. But, this change took a while to occur and only happened after a lot of pushing, practising and adjusting what I was doing. Importantly…

'PULL' OPPORTUNITIES ONLY START TO HAPPEN WHEN YOU'VE SUCCESSFULLY CREATED SOME 'PUSH' OPPORTUNITIES AND THEN *PROVED YOURSELF*

When you eventually manage to create a situation where you start to get pull opportunities arriving on your doorstep (and especially if they're related to what you want to do and where your happiness lies) then you'll be in the hugely privileged and exciting position of being able to choose to do what you *really* want to do every day.

And as you know, I strongly believe that a large part of being 'successful' is doing what brings you happiness and fulfilment, every single day.

Now, once you've made opportunities arise, you then encounter the final phase of the 'F.O.C. It' process…

CHOICES are what happen when you land (or create) more than one opportunity, be they 'push' or 'pull' ones. Then, you're in the fabulous position of being able to choose which opportunities to take. Sometimes you'll know right away which ones to go for, and sometimes it's useful to enlist the advice of wise people around you. In any case, the luxury of 'choice' is something to be treasured and when an opportunity does arise, you should give it considerable thought, because opportunities are your chance to create *even more* exciting opportunities and ultimately eventually reach the long-term goals you're shooting for.

So now you can use the concept of 'F.O.C. It' – Focus, Opportunities and Choices, to mould your life and the lives of others – and, in fact, you can say to anyone you meet...

'GO F.O.C. YOURSELF!'

SECRET 16
WHAT'S YOUR STORY?

You and I have our own, very personal, definitions of what 'success' actually is. And, in fact, everyone has a slightly different view. That's why you could say I'm not being that brave by calling this book *Success Or Your Money Back*, because success can be defined so widely. One person's definition of success may be another person's normal, day-to-day life...and that person's measure of success may be yet another person's complete and utter nightmare!

YOU...AND YOUR SUCCESS

I often think about success and how I define it. 'Success' for you takes on a very personal form. Here's one of my goals:

TO BE A GOOD DINNER PARTY GUEST

For me, the richest, most successful people are those who can make choices and those who have the best stories. For me, the decision to embark on any project partly relates to whether it's ever been done before, partly to whether it will make me test myself (because you *always* grow when you push yourself into unfamiliar situations), partly if it amuses me and also, to a large extent, whether I think it might be a fantastic adventure – and make a great story to recount and look back on.

One measure of 'success' goes like this:

WEALTH IS NOT ABOUT HAVING THE MOST MONEY

IT'S ABOUT HAVING THE BEST STORIES TO TELL

I always think about being invited to a dinner party, or even to Buckingham Palace (still waiting for the invite, sure it's coming soon!), and try to imagine what sort of guest I'd be. Of course, it's impolite to talk about yourself all the time, but if you *are* asked about yourself, then it's good to be able to engage those around you and be a human who enriches or entertains others in your vicinity. When you're on your deathbed, looking back on your life, surely it'll be your wish to have lived your life to the very fullest? And when you're alive, isn't it best to be both interesting and positive to those around you? Sometimes, there's a lot of pressure from 'society' to be wealthy. But being *rich in experiences* and *obscenely loaded with positivity* are also admirable (and arguably better) goals.

'STORIES' CAN HELP YOU, TOO

The concept of having and creating 'stories' is also important if you ever find yourself in a situation where you want others to notice what you're doing at any point in your life. People connect with stories – and this is crucial, especially if you're trying to get media attention. In common parlance, the act of striving to get noticed is often called 'marketing' or 'publicity'.

YOU MUST TELL A STORY

If you want journalists and bloggers to write about you, and thus the wider world to know about what you do, it's often not good enough to 'just' have a brilliant product, you need a good STORY around it, too…

When I self-published my novelty blank book *What Every Man Thinks About Apart From Sex*, I was delighted with the end result and felt it deserved attention. This is a very common emotion when you've created something new. You think to yourself…*'I know what I've made is great, so I'm sure everyone else will think it's great, too – and they'll be sure to report on it simply existing.'* You believe that the very fact that your idea has come to life deems it worthy of being reported to the world.

But, actually, for something to become 'news', it's usually not enough for something 'new' to have simply been created.

Can you imagine this headline?..

NEW PRODUCT RELEASED FROM
NON-FAMOUS PERSON OR COMPANY

Hmm…not so likely.

Maybe if you're 'technology giant' Apple Inc, it's enough to just tell everyone about your latest product, but even then they wrap a story around the launch of a new product – *'This will change the way you use your phone'* for example – but for most of us who are trying to be heard among millions of others, it's always beneficial to highlight a story behind your product.

When I launched *What Every Man Thinks About Apart From Sex*, it wasn't the product itself – or the fact that it was totally blank inside – that got reported on around the world. Rather, it was the detail that students were using the book as a notepad during lectures. Then later, after the first wave of publicity, journalists reported on the fact that an entirely blank book had reached number forty-four in the Amazon book chart.

People weren't reporting on the product coming out per se, they were reporting on what *happened* when the product came out…a very important and crucial distinction. Humans love stories.

And it's also vitally important that you…

BRING YOUR STORY TO LIFE

You can wonderfully bring your story to life with one or more *good quality* IMAGES. The saying goes that 'a picture is worth a thousand words'. I'd argue that these days, it's worth way, way more! With the internet being such an amazing tool to spread and share ideas, a good picture can be worth a thousand clicks, sometimes a million, because people can share it so easily and quickly.

But, quality is important. I would always recommend that you make sure that the images you send out to accompany your story are of a good standard: simply shot, evenly lit, in focus, against a plain background. This will then draw the eye only to what you're trying to show, and create a finished image that makes your whole story come to life in a professional way. This then allows professionals who care about what they do (and have a very large reach) to include your content in their output.

One trick I've learned for getting good-quality images created cheaply is to utilise the amazing service that many high-street photo developers offer. These places often have a very small studio area already set up with professional cameras, industry-quality lights and a plain background. In fact, some health stores also often have pre-set photography areas to take 'mother and baby' photos. These mini portable studios can be perfect for creating press shots because they're ready to go and often the person operating them is very skilled. So, the images you end up with are pin sharp, well lit and very reasonably priced.

Another great way to bring your story to life, so you can get people to write about it, is with a short video clip. These days, you can create a video cheaply and upload it to YouTube right away. By shooting your video on a tripod (so there's no 'camera shake') and ensuring it's well lit and has decent quality sound, you'll maximise the chance that you'll communicate your message and that others will include it on their websites. If you give your video a title that's carefully created to relate to the key element of your story, then when any person or journalist searches for your story on a search engine, they'll find your video too (because Google automatically embeds YouTube videos in their search results). This will be hugely useful in spreading the word about your story in general but, pivotally, allows bloggers to easily discover your video and then include it in their articles, making it even more attractive for them to write about you. By making your video and images easily accessible, it's then very easy for anyone to create a slick, layered and interesting piece about your story.

So, no matter how good an idea is before you're about to launch, it's definitely worth spending time and effort to find the story behind it. Whether it's about the product or service itself, you the creator of it or the journey to get it made – get it down in writing and hopefully it'll engage people. By also providing images and videos with what you've written, you'll then give anyone interested in reporting on your news, the resources and ability to do so easily and quickly. Then, the story of your launch will be much more likely to have a very happy and successful ending.

SECRET 17
THE 33% RULE

This is a mind trick that helps if doubt ever crosses your mind when you're planning to send something out into the world that you've recently created (and pretty much all of us are anxious about doing so).

Here's the 33% rule:

Roughly 33% of people will *love* what you do.

Roughly 33% of people will *hate* what you do.

Roughly 33% of people will *not care* what you do.

No matter *what* you produce, be it the *Mona Lisa*, Beethoven's Fifth, a Michelin-starred meal, the Sistine Chapel...not EVERY SINGLE PERSON will ever agree that what you've done is *amazing*.

This is actually great news and very empowering, because once you realise that there's no absolute standard for anything that's been created by a human, it frees you up to go with your best judgement when you make something new and to then look forward to finding out if some of the world likes what you do and, if so, how many people will actually engage with it.

Humans are INCREDIBLY COMPLEX and varied, so their reactions aren't always logical, and they're *never, ever* unanimous. Because we've all had different pasts, and thus we each have different views of the world based on those pasts, every person will react differently to anything they encounter. And that includes everything you produce, too.

So, if you're ever feeling anxious about launching something you've created to a wider audience, you must always remember the 33% rule and try to build some armour by using that knowledge because...

YOU ARE A SENSITIVE SOUL

The truth is, most people are affected by the reactions, feelings and feedback of others. It's good that we are (people who *aren't* are called 'psychopaths'!) because these feelings make us care about others. Sometimes we take on board what's fed to us from the outside and it hurts when someone says something negative about what we do – and we tend to take it personally.

This is a difficult situation to deal with, because sometimes you need to listen to other people's feedback, as they'll have a constructive point of view. But, you need to...

FILTER WHO AFFECTS YOU

By using the 33% rule when you launch anything into the world, you'll then instantly expect 33% negativity, just as the sun will rise tomorrow. You'll also be unsurprised when 33% of the people display total apathy after finding out about what you've done, just as the world is round (at least, the scientists and NASA images currently tell us it is, anyway). And the brighter news is that you can also look forward to the 33% who will like what you do. And you can then FOCUS ON THIS 33%. They could be any, or possibly all, of the following:

FERVENT SUPPORTERS

FUTURE LOVERS

POSSIBLE PARTNERS

CUSTOMERS

Once you lock it into your brain that it is HUMANLY IMPOSSIBLE for every single person to like what you do, it's entirely liberating, because then you'll be less apprehensive about telling others your ideas and also less surprised or hurt when you encounter someone who doesn't like one of your suggestions or creations…

And remember also that…

WE ARE ALL MERE BLIPS IN THE UNIVERSE

Granted, some of us are slightly 'blippier' blips in the grand scheme of things but, nevertheless, every one of us will eventually still pass into the vast history of time. So, if you can, remember that the only person that really matters is YOU, try to stop worrying about what people will think and just have a go at something new.

SECRET 18
TREAT YOUR LIFE LIKE AN EXPERIMENT

The mind boggles. When you stop to think that you and I could have been born at any time in human history (or even not at all!) then it's pretty amazing that we're alive today during such wonderful leaps forward in human endeavour.

We are INCREDIBLY FORTUNATE in so many ways to be living at this time of world history. It's pretty mind-blowing when you think about it – we could have been born in the Stone Age, the Renaissance or even during the relatively recent World Wars. In fact, we could have existed in any other seventy-year section along the enormous timeline in which people have existed.

Instead, we've been born into the world right at this specific time in human existence, and we're living at an amazing time, too. The medical advances, the phenomenal opportunities that the internet now gives us, and the wondrous amount of human creativity around us, all make our lives longer, richer and more enjoyable. But there's one thing that's really wrong, and I'd go as far as to say that in one major respect…

WE'RE DEEPLY UNCIVILISED

There's something very wrong with how we treat young people and with how we educate our young. Virtually all schools across the world operate a 'pass and fail' system and this drums into us the (deeply damaging) idea that:

'FAILURE IS BAD'

Therefore, people grow up trying to avoid failure, rather than trying numerous avenues to succeed. And thus, many people don't even start something new for fear of failing.

The reality is that:

'FAILURE IS GOOD'

Because it very clearly and directly signifies you're trying something new.

In a hundred years, or even sooner, I think we'll teach young people differently. We'll teach them about how to make things happen, entrepreneurship, how to be a decent human, the skills needed to be a great parent and how to live a creative and fulfilled life – rather than how to mostly pass tests.

And one way I like to trick my brain into trying new things is to think of my life as an 'experiment'. It's a neat trick that immediately reframes everything you do, because:

EXPERIMENTS NEVER 'FAIL'

When a scientist sets up an experiment, the scientist follows a strict structure of 'hypothesis, method, results and conclusion'. As you know, the hypothesis is what the scientist *believes* (or often, hopes) will happen at the end of the experiment, the 'method' is how the scientist goes about completing the experiment and the 'results' are what the scientist observes happening when the experiment is run. In the 'conclusion', the scientist then reviews what happened during the experiment and decides two things: whether the original hypothesis (belief) was correct and whether to conduct another experiment based on what was learned in the first experiment. This next experiment might then have a different method and end with even more different and interesting results.

The important point to note is that, no matter what happens during the experiment, as long as something *does* happen, then the experiment is deemed to be a success – simply because it got results, whether those results confirm the scientist's original belief or throw up new possibilities and avenues to conduct another experiment. And the next experiment might well bring that scientist closer to their goal, or give them ideas for an even more exciting and different goal. The fantastic upshot is:

EXPERIMENTS *ALWAYS* GET RESULTS

What's more, the fantastic fact about the concept of 'experimentation' is that when you experiment, sometimes you get an even better result than you hoped for. In the scientific world, when Marie Curie was looking into photography, she actually discovered radioactivity. Her experiment wasn't viewed as a 'failure' in the field of photography; instead it was viewed as a huge success (and a gigantic scientific breakthrough) in the realm of understanding radioactivity.

So, it's enormously empowering to know that…

IF YOU VIEW YOUR LIFE LIKE AN EXPERIMENT, THEN… YOU'LL NEVER FAIL

Which is a great thought isn't it!

SECRET 19
GENERATION FORTUNATE

At this point, you and I should really say a general, all-encompassing *'Thank You.com'* into the ether of the universe. We need to add the '.com' part because, during our lifetime, we've been fortunate enough to have been born during a period in human development when a hugely significant leap forward in communication has occurred, namely the internet. Not only does the net allow us to connect easily with others and share ideas, it allows us to quickly find experts who can help us achieve whatever we desire.

For me though, one of the most thrilling aspects of the net – which sends chills down my spine every time I think about it – is that...

THERE ARE NO BARRIERS TO STOP YOU REACHING BILLIONS OF PEOPLE

In the past, the wealthy few who controlled the 'means of communication' held enormous power. If you owned a printing press, then you had the ability to create documents that could reach large numbers of people, the 'masses'. But printing presses were expensive to build and run, so only the very wealthy people that owned them had a voice, and those who didn't, had to ask permission to use the press. The same goes for the other great leaps forward in human communication, radio and T.V. The ability to reach others through these media was still blocked by decision makers who decided what should be printed or broadcast.

Now though, with the internet, that power is democratised in the most beautifully, powerfully 'socialist' way. Not only can every single one of us have a voice, because you can easily upload anything you write or produce, we also have the potential for that voice to be heard by billions of people WITHOUT ANYONE'S PERMISSION.

For someone like myself who believes in the monumentally magnificent value of individually unique humans, coupled with the fact that I also like anything that disrupts the conventional way of doing things, this makes the internet one of the most exciting developments imaginable. The end result of having the web is that pretty much anyone (or at least, those of us fortunate to live in a free society) can potentially reach a huge audience with a few clicks – and that's simply thrilling, stupendous and breathtaking. On the web, there are no barriers – count them: NONE – to putting up content that potentially millions and millions of people can see.

It's pretty cool that…

NO ONE CAN TELL YOU 'NO'

And if you're a doer, who wants to make things happen, that's incredibly empowering. So, you and I should feel very fortunate to be living at a time when we can find any expert to help us reach our goals and also have the ability to communicate our ideas to the world, both with just a couple of clicks.

SECRET 20
KNOWLEDGE IS DEAD

I'm sure you know the expression that says:

KNOWLEDGE IS POWER

Well, hold the front page and move over 'knowledge'. Because, in this amazing time we live in, knowledge is no longer power. In fact, due to the phenomenal presence of the internet, knowledge is very easy to find.

KNOWLEDGE IS CHEAP

These days, the wonderful World Wide Web allows us to find information very quickly and easily. And this means that conventional wisdom about 'knowledge' has been turned on its head. So, *stand clear of the doors and hold small children by the hand*, because this ride is going to get bumpy…

KNOWLEDGE IS NO LONGER 'POWER'

There's a new guy in town…

CREATIVITY IS THE NEW POWER

Because there's so much information at your keyboard-tapping fingertips, knowledge is no longer difficult to come by. But, due to this knowledge being available to everyone, simply having it in your brain can't easily give you a competitive edge. And there's another curious effect that the internet has on the power dynamic of innovation and ideas. When a new idea is launched, because of the way information is now spread so easily everyone else can instantly see that idea. Therefore, this means it's even more vital for anyone wanting to have any edge at all to keep new ideas coming at a regular and fast pace, because it's likely that any 'old' ideas will be copied, tweaked or refined very soon after they're released.

Henry Ford, creator of the modern motor car, once said that he didn't need to 'clutter up' his mind with 'general knowledge', as long as he had the resources around him to supply any knowledge he required and, in *his* time, that resource was the team of amazing people who he hired. Today, each of us doesn't need a team of brilliant advisors; we have the web, a ready-made knowledge bank where we can find out pretty much anything in the blink of an eye. Ford's principles of keeping an 'uncluttered mind' while knowing where to find answers still stands today, but what's even more important than 'knowledge' now is *how* we use it to allow us to create something new and exciting – and also to get our creations out into the world for people to engage with them.

The internet has vastly speeded up human development, because we can all learn from each other much faster now and instantly see what's possible. Sometimes, just knowing what's possible can change everything. It took years and years before athletes could break the four-minute barrier for running a mile, and yet, when one man – Roger Bannister – did, others quickly broke it too. The knowledge that something *can* be done, immediately frees up a goal that everyone previously thought to be impossible – and then many others find they can achieve that 'impossible' feat, too.

So, never worry that you don't have enough knowledge. Thanks to the amazing internet, knowledge today is cheap, speedily available and often free. What's now really valuable is how you make connections between existing knowledge in order to create something new...

SECRET 21
THE DRUNK LIFE

Our DEMONS have a lot to answer for. A huge amount of both our happiness and success in our lives is down to us battling the internal voices that try to limit us. These destructive inner monologues arise from our past experiences, from growing up – and from our parents and teachers, too – and they're often very hard to banish. They're the little voices in our head that say 'NO', 'YOU CAN'T' or 'YOU'RE NOT GOOD ENOUGH'. Our demons sometimes speak to us in a silent, often subconscious way and they're frequently responsible for us making bad life decisions or deciding against embarking on new goals.

One demon that limits many people is the worry of how others will see us, and the '33% Rule' is helpful to deal with this, because it makes you more ready for what'll happen whenever you raise your head above the parapet and push yourself or your ideas out into the world. But, it's always good to have another mental tool in your armoury that'll help fight this very powerful and damaging mental gremlin:

THE 'WHAT PEOPLE MAY THINK' DEMON

As social animals, we care about what others think of us. That's just natural. But sometimes this concern about how others will view us stops us from doing things we might otherwise want to do. What we really need to do then, is…

BANISH THE DEMONS

Now, a curious human condition is that when we drink alcohol, one of the results is that our inhibitions are lowered. Drunk people worry much less about how they'll be viewed and they don't think nearly as deeply about the consequences of their actions as they'd normally do when sober. (I'm sure you can recall vivid memories of friends or relatives doing something outrageous or embarrassing while 'under the influence'. You're probably conjuring up one such memory right now…)

LIVE YOUR LIFE LIKE YOU'RE DRUNK…

Imagine what you'd be like if you made all your life decisions as if you were drunk. We all know that imbibing alcohol makes most people much more *fearless*, *impulsive* and *spontaneous*. And in general life, those traits are the same ones that can often lead to exciting adventures happening and new achievements being reached.

Now, I'm not for a moment suggesting you should go to your local bar and start buying up the entire inventory so that you can suddenly start being incredibly fearless and wildly successful. When someone is drunk, their judgement can often get impaired *too much* and there are the obvious health risks too, of course. It's not a good idea to go through life 'numb' or totally disconnected from reality, but it is still a very helpful mental exercise to consider what demons might be limiting you at any point in your life and to ask yourself this question when you're deciding whether to embark on something new:

'WHAT WOULD I DO IF I WERE DRUNK RIGHT NOW?'

This mind trick makes you focus on whether you, or your demons, are in control – and whether those demons are making you just a little bit too inhibited, or stopping you from doing something that you should just simply have a go at making happen. The 'reality' people experience when drunk is a slightly different reality to when they're sober – and this is the crucial point. The reality we have in our mind at any given point determines what decisions we make at that point too. And rather than trying to imagine how another (hopefully wildly successful and happy) person would think, which is hard, it's easier to think how you'd act if your fear barrier was lowered just a little bit.

So, maybe if you were to live life like you're drunk, but without the actual drinking, incredible adventures might follow.

PERHAPS WE ALL JUST NEED A BIT MORE BOTTLE...

SECRET 22
BE INSPIRED IN AN INSTANT

In order to come up with great new ideas, you need to give your brain the chance to have an exciting 'ah ha!' moment. The good news is that...

INSPIRATION CAN COME FROM PRETTY MUCH EVERYWHERE

Every single one of your life experiences gets pasted into your 'Mental Scrapbook' (not an official part of the anatomy, but a newly discovered area of grey matter identified by 'Dr Simove'), the astonishing part of your brain that you draw on when you're thinking up new ideas. Everything you see, smell, touch, taste and feel gets deposited here – and the contents of your Mental Scrapbook are then drawn upon when you're coming up with any new plan or concept. Importantly, the past experiences in your Mental Scrapbook will also affect *how* you'll make any idea happen. That's why two people will never bring an idea to life in the exact same way.

It's wonderfully reassuring to know that every single experience in your past is potentially useful, so the more knowledge and experience you can stick into your Mental Scrapbook, the better. Whatever goes into your brain will allow you to start mining what's inside your head in order to come up with ideas and to make them happen too.

In order to be creative, it's helpful to coax your mind into going down certain specific avenues, otherwise it can be pretty overwhelming to just try to *start thinking up an idea*. Now, what I keep my eyes and ears open for, and tend to use a lot, are…

TRIGGERS

A trigger can be anything that focuses your mind to launch from a particular subject area and go down a route that'll help you come up with great ideas. Mental triggers are such a fabulous tool because they give your mind a springboard to begin from and they make the whole 'idea creation' process so much more manageable and way less daunting.

The best triggers are anything that stimulates your mind to have a thought that, when combined with the secrets I'll outline soon, allows you to come up with a new idea or method for anything you're trying to do.

You can find these triggers around your home, outside on the street, on the net, pretty much anywhere really. As long as you're open to the idea that anything you encounter can be a trigger, then you'll begin to discover them everywhere. However, sometimes you'll want an easy-to-reach source which is enormously rich in a wide variety of these helpful sparks, so that you can get a lot more done in a single hit and become inspired way more quickly.

A one-stop-shop that's great for triggers is a MUSEUM. This is because museums are usually full of objects and stories from a wide variety of human existence. When you're trying to come up with a new thought or strategy, all the different artefacts and showcases in any museum can force you to look at something from a fresh, sideways perspective – and when you link them to the situation you're in, that'll often be enough to trigger a fantastic new idea in your brain.

The 'portable museum'

I'm well aware that it may not be entirely possible for us to wander around museums all day, trying to get inspired. So, a more practical solution is to use a 'portable museum' in the form of an encyclopaedia. A good encyclopaedia can do a similar job as a museum by making you encounter a variety of stimuli that, when coupled with your unique experience, will get your brain firing on all cylinders and coming up with new concepts or solutions for anything you're working on. And a great bonus about a book (or even an encyclopaedia on a computer) is that you can easily keep it near you, ready for whenever you need to be inspired. If you repeatedly open an encyclopaedia at random pages, you'll start to find the variety of content you encounter becomes a fantastic mental springboard.

You'll soon find that all the pictures and entries in the encyclopaedia will start to spark your grey matter. For example, if you were to open the encyclopaedia on a page that showed an entry for 'Ancient Egypt', your mind might well immediately start to think of pyramids, slave labour, sand and hieroglyphics. If you mentally focus on all these elements one by one, and then apply them to any situation for which you want to come up with a new idea or strategy, you'll be surprised that they might immediately begin to suggest to you new ways for approaching any goal you're trying to reach.

For example, if I was trying to think of an original present for a loved one, and I stumbled across a page on Ancient Egypt, I might start thinking about creating a personalized 'pyramid' out of their favourite chocolates or writing them a poem on paper that looked like ancient papyrus. And if I was trying to think of a new service for a banking business, I might take inspiration from the idea that 'many people' made building the Pharaohs' tombs possible, so perhaps we could harness the power of everyone who has an account with the bank to do something equally impressive, like raise a huge amount for a charity or invest in new businesses so that everyone's risk was tiny, but collectively the fund would be enormous. Or, I might think about how in Ancient Egypt, many people believed in an 'afterlife' – this might get me thinking of a promotion for pensions or inheritance insurance…

As you can tell, these example ideas aren't yet fully formed, but you can instantly see how the technique of using an encyclopaedia as a springboard can start to work. The important thing is that whatever goal you're trying to achieve, you can ALWAYS find inspiration for solutions you need from triggers like the ones you'll find in a museum or encyclopaedia.

Four-legged inspiration

Here's another great source of triggers. In horse racing, horses are given the most unusual, random names – and these can send your mind in exciting new directions. As you scan your eyes down the horses' names below, imagine that right now you're trying to come up with a new product or an original solution for a business…and view the horses' names simply as a starting point. These are some real horses' names I found just after a quick look in a betting newspaper that I bought for precisely this purpose:

Mystical Magician

Blaze King

Grand Vision

As you read each one, let it sink into your mind for a second – and then think about the possible ways the horse's name could lead you to a new idea or strategy. Perhaps 'Mystical Magician' might immediately make you think of 'theatres', 'illusions', 'tricks', or even 'rabbits'. And 'Grand Vision' might make you think of 'seeing things more clearly', 'eyes', 'spectacles', 'a big overview' or even 'a thousand'. All these quick associations are like little sparks to fire your ideas engine, and if you follow the train of thought they each trigger, they could well give you your next fantastic brainwave.

Triggers are everywhere and can come from surprising sources. Once, whilst driving along a motorway, I heard someone on the radio utter a famous phrase, and the words smashed into my consciousness. *'Well...of course...money can't buy happiness...'* the voice said. Bam! My brain was triggered and instantly exploded with ideas. I started to wonder whether I could actually make a product called 'HAPPINESS' and then sell it. By turning the famous phrase on its head, perhaps I could create a fun new gift in the process. I swiftly teamed up with a fantastic gift wholesaler and, a few months later, the finished product was ready – a shiny metal key chain that spelt the word 'Happiness' and also doubled as a bottle opener. The finished item was a triumph, giving anyone the chance to finally 'buy happiness...' And it all started with an unexpected trigger...

The brilliant thing about triggers (and the techniques coming up, as well) is that the more you use them, the more naturally you'll think of ideas. And soon, you'll find it easier to make connections and be inspired. Plus, it should take less conscious effort, because your subconscious will automatically start to do these tricks for you whenever you're awake (and sometimes when you're asleep, too!). So, in effect, ideas will then just start popping into your head.

When they do, just make sure you quickly write them down and then come back to them later, in order to decide which ones to set into motion right away.

SECRET 23
HOW TO UNLOCK THE AMAZING IDEAS INSIDE YOU

Many people view the ability to come up with new and innovative ideas as something 'innate' or 'magical'. I often hear people say:

'OH BUT I'M NOT CREATIVE!'

Well, I'm here to categorically tell you that creativity is not actually a shady 'dark art' that only some people are born with – or a skill the most talented practitioners can learn. In fact, every single human being can be creative and I've got some easy tricks that will help anyone come up with new and exciting ideas. I use them all the time and firmly believe that creativity can be learned. It's just a series of techniques.

I'M IN LOVE WITH YOUR BRAIN

Your brain is the sexiest organ in your body. I know this because no matter how gorgeous your face looks, how flat your stomach is – or how perfect your beautiful behind may be, your brain has the ability to make ANYTHING happen. And that's hugely sexy! The reason your brain is such an astonishing organ is very simple. It evolved over millions of years to be a brilliant problem-solving device. And 'creativity' is really just problem solving in its rawest form.

Unlike any other animal brain on Earth (or computer for that matter) your human brain has evolved into an amazing tool that can do three remarkable things:

IMAGINE...CREATE...AND PLAN

Not only can your brain think up an idea that hasn't happened yet (which is pretty WOW when you think about it!), it can also come up with the solutions to make that idea happen (HANDY!), and then carry out a plan to do so (SUPERB!).

No other animal on Earth can do this like us humans. And sometimes, we need to be reminded that the pulsating mound of jelly in our skulls has enormous power. This muscle has developed into something so phenomenal because, since life began, all animals have needed to come up with ways to find food, shelter and a mate. And so our brains have evolved to allow us to find ways to do all those things very well. It just so happens that the same skills needed to provide a meal, a roof and a companion are also transferable in terms of making anything you want happen.

Because we've got such great brains – which are naturally built to solve problems – once you engage with a very simple process, you're very likely to achieve success. The process goes like this:

IDEA + ACTION = ADVENTURE

OR = PROFIT

OR = HAPPINESS

That's pretty empowering when you think about it. Every human achievement has come from an idea in someone's head, coupled with their actions – or the actions of anyone else they got to help them with their goal.

Now, the first step is the IDEA, and the following three techniques are the ones that I use to come up with original concepts. They're like 'idea cheats' really, and once you see how easy they are, it's like pulling back the curtain on the Wizard Of Oz's creativity's booth and seeing that the workings inside are actually quite simple and easily achievable.

SECRET 24
TWIST SOMETHING ALREADY EXISTING

It's a common misconception that new ideas come right out of the blue or that they result from wildly left-field, original thoughts that no one else has ever dreamed up.

NOT TRUE

First, there are more than six billion brains in the world (and even more that have been active in the past), so it's likely that one or more of those brains may well have come up with a certain specific idea before.

Second, even if an idea has indeed been thought of previously, if no one has put that idea into practice (by actioning it), it won't actually have come to life. Most 'new ideas' are often not that far removed from existing ideas; they've just been updated in some clever way, so that the end result is different from what has gone before. And that's what's important – that's what makes them 'new'.

Clocking off

Here's a very small-scale example from my life. I wanted to create a fun new gift that office workers might want to buy during the 'Secret Santa' gift-giving season that happens over the Christmas period. As you probably know, 'Secret Santa' is a mainly office-based tradition whereby each team member buys a co-worker a surprise gift up to a certain value, which is often rather low.

I began to think about the workplace in general and how it's often common for people in offices to watch their clocks while they yearn for the end of the working day. (*'Workers of the world unite! You have nothing to lose but your chains'*, I holler!) So, I began to think about how I could take something already existing, a clock, and alter it slightly to give me a 'new' type of clock. I decided to create a clock with only two numerals on the face – the five and six, and add some wording to the middle of the clock that read 'It's Nearly Home Time'. I called my creation 'The Optimistic Office Clock'. The accumulated effect of the two numerals and the wording meant that even though the hands might be pointing to the correct time, throughout the working day, because only the 'five' and 'six' numerals were showing, it would seem like the clock had an inbuilt optimistic viewpoint that the time was always *nearly* five or six o'clock, the hours when most people in an office leave to go home.

WHERE'S MY NOBEL PRIZE?

The 'Optimistic Office Clock' will hardly change the world, but this example of creativity neatly shows how updating or twisting something already existing means you can instantly become creative and produce something that people see as new or different.

The next creativity secret is a fun one…

SECRET 25
BREAK A RULE

The rules around us are fascinating. They're how we humans organise ourselves at this point in time, hopefully with the aim to be 'civilised' or to make the system work. I often think that in a hundred years' time, many of the rules we have today might be different. So what does that make us now? Wrong? Or just 'doing our best' perhaps? The important point is that when someone tells you something HAS to be done the way it is because it's a rule, or even that it's 'always been done that way', then you should see this as a wonderful flashing beacon that shows you an opportunity to be creative by producing something new that everyone else who follows the rule would never do.

Sometimes, when you closely examine something that people around you – and you – think is a rule that cannot be broken, it unravels like a cheap sweater.

AT THIS POINT I HOPE YOU WON'T MIND IF I NOW THANK MY MUM, IF THAT'S OKAY

THANK YOU MUM

My mother gave me many gifts in life and one of them was a challenging view of the world that can be summed up in one word:

'WHY?'

When I was growing up, I heard my mother ask '*Why?*' a lot, and now I realise that this tiny but mighty word has the power both to create new ideas and change the world too.

IF YOU QUESTION EVERYTHING AND ASK:

'WHY IS IT LIKE THAT?'

THEN YOU OFTEN COME UP WITH NEW SOLUTIONS FOR HOW SOMETHING COULD BE...

Asking '*Why?*' is a great method for breaking rules because often, when you find out the reason for a rule (or established tradition or way of working), it frequently throws up amazing possibilities of how things can change.

Asking '*Why?*' also gives rise to an equally powerful question that you can also use in your arsenal when you're battling towards success:

'WHY NOT?'

Even though *'WHY NOT?'* can be a good question to ask, especially when someone is challenging you on why you think an idea is good, sometimes you have to be a little bit careful when using it. When you're trying to reach a new goal, many people (and sometimes yourself) will be all too happy to answer your question *'WHY NOT?'* with many reasons why you shouldn't carry out a particular plan. And that's not always hugely helpful. However, if you ask *'WHY NOT?'* when you're in a situation deciding whether to start something, and it leaves you (or anyone else you're with) shrugging your shoulders and saying, *'Yeah...right...why not!'* then that is most certainly positive and energising.

WHO MAKES THE RULES?

Sometimes when you start researching a 'rule', you'll discover it's not as unbreakable as you might have thought. Day to day, many of us make *assumptions* about the world around us (and even about our own inner world of possibilities too), and that's because of our life experiences and conditioning. This is why it's always wonderfully refreshing to hear a child's ideas, because a young mind hasn't yet learned the way things are 'meant to be'.

The truth of the matter is that *nothing* is 'meant to be'. Humans have only created rules and traditions with the aim of making society better (or arguably, to control others). And sometimes the definition of 'better' changes from one person to another – what might be better for the rule-makers might not be better for you. And in human history, all our laws, norms, traditions, taboos and beliefs have changed in differing amounts from century to century. So, one thing is for sure, CHANGE always happens. And that's why when we find ourselves thinking *'it has to be done in a certain way'*, we should stop ourselves, ask *'WHY?'* and then see if in fact, any 'rule' we're considering following, could be done differently without the world collapsing.

Money for nothing

Once, I heard about an amazing phenomenon that led me to break a rule – or at least, something I *thought* was a rule when I started out…

It all began when I read about a situation on the internet that blew me away. People had been playing a popular online game you might have heard of, called 'Second Life'. This game allows users to create a character and enter a virtual online world, complete with other virtual people, virtual buildings and – amazingly – its very own virtual currency. The 'Second Life' currency is called Linden Dollars, named after Linden Lab, the real-world company that created the game.

Now, what rocked my world was not that the currency existed in the online game, but that I learned it was being traded on eBay for 'real-world' money. I blinked hard as I looked at auction listings showing Linden Dollars being traded for actual U.S. dollars. Here was a 'virtual currency' that could only be used inside a computer game, being sold for real money outside the computer game – incredible! Something that only 'existed' as computer code (or graphics on a screen) was been given actual, real 'value'. To me, this seemed like money was being created out of thin air.

It also got me thinking about the whole concept of 'money' and how we buy, sell and allocate 'value' in our society. I remembered a black-and-white photograph I'd seen when I was eighteen years old, showing a man during the Great Depression. During this time in the 1930s, the economy of the world crashed, and inflation grew to such an extent that money began to lose its worth (a situation that's hard to get your head around, because we take it for granted that the money in our pockets will *always* be worth what we expect it to be worth). The photograph I'd seen was a man pushing a cart stacked full of banknotes. He needed that huge amount of cash just to buy a loaf of bread because the currency had become so devalued.

I began to think hard about a question that had always bothered me: *'How can money lose its worth?'* I started to focus in on the (rather worrying) reality that the money in our pockets is simply a 'promise', and that each note or coin holds no real value in its physical form – it's actually just cheap paper or metal. Even the money in our banks is really just a number on a computer screen that relates to some physical entity that the bank or governments have in their possession, and that we hope will hold its value. Moreover, the value of money is set by governments, bodies and economic forces, which most of us can't affect.

We only accept the use of money because we all believe money has a value. In a way, our daily use of cash is a shared delusion, or at least an active agreement between all of us to share the delusion. A 'conscious delusion' – rather priceless!

Of course, most worldwide currencies are backed by actual gold reserves but, there again, gold is only deemed valuable because there's a fixed amount of it in the world and, importantly, people want it. If, suddenly, the state of the economy meant that the money in our pockets became virtually worthless, you and I could do nothing about it. When I think about this, I suddenly have a massive urge to turn all of my hard-earned cash into solid gold bars. But that's not enormously practical when buying your groceries in the local supermarket – and of course, that's the reason why paper money was created.

All this began to make me think about the whole concept of 'value' and how something only has value if us humans think it does, and agree it does. And this whole area of 'perceived value' relates to another question that has also always intrigued me:

HOW MUCH IS A PIECE OF MODERN ART WORTH?

When many people look at an intricately painted 'Old Master' or a respected piece of historical art, (such as the *Mona Lisa*) most people (but still not ALL) will agree that the skill involved in creating that painting and, also that the end result of that skill, the painting itself, has considerable value. However, it's still very interesting to consider why certain paintings have such higher value (in society) than others – they might be valuable because they're famous, and yet they might be famous because they've been deemed valuable. Intriguing!

Now, for the general observer, it's much more difficult to rationalise why some pieces of modern art are deemed to have enormous worth. A casual observer looking at 'a work of art' consisting of some neon tubes lying on the floor, half a shark placed in a tank, or even a conventional light switch placed in a picture frame, might indeed find it hard to believe that they are worth thousands, or hundreds of thousands. Sometimes, when people view modern art, they say *'I could have done that'*. And the answer given by the art establishment is usually *'But you didn't!'*

This brings up the question of *who* decides what's defined as modern art and what isn't. Is something only modern art when a 'modern artist' creates it or if it's shown in an art gallery?

As a person whose whole life is focused on creating, I've come to realise that it's not always the time it takes to actually *make* something that's important, it's often the time (and experience) it took to create the thought that started the original idea, which eventually led to the final creation coming to life, that's crucial. But of course, these factors are much less visible in the finished creation of a modern art piece, than say, the artistry of a brushstroke or the realistic nature of a painted portrait. And that's why many of us deem modern art as having much less – or no – value.

All these thoughts about the 'shifting sands of value' led me to one question that I thought might be related to a strict rule:

CAN YOU PRINT YOUR OWN MONEY?

Now, when this idea popped into my head, I first thought that it was illegal to create your own currency. I believed that a 'rule' in our world existed to prohibit this action and that breaking the rule would result in punishment. Then, I started looking into the rule I'd assumed and quickly discovered that, yes, it's highly illegal to print your own versions of someone else's currency (it's commonly called 'banknote fraud'!) but actually, it's not at all illegal to print your own, totally new currency. In fact, most large high-street stores and brands print their own currency, they're just called a different name: VOUCHERS. These vouchers are still traded for goods, just like 'real' money, the only difference is that vouchers – or coupons – can only be used in specific stores or to buy specific goods owned by the issuing companies.

So, armed with the new knowledge that printing a currency wasn't actually illegal and fired by this freeing realisation, I immediately drew up some sketches for my very own money. I decided to call my currency 'The Ego', because it both sounded like a real currency and it also related to the enormous chutzpah of releasing my own banknote. I found some amazing graphic designers to help me, and the finished EGO banknote not only came out looking wonderfully authentic, it actually sold online (and still does to this day). This meant that I'd given something with little value, a much greater value than the actual materials it was made from – and that I'd successfully printed and released my own currency.

Moreover, I'd discovered that sometimes when you think a rule blocks your way, actually if you dig a bit deeper you might find the rule isn't actually a rule, or that there's a way around it...

The last secret I'll describe for coming up with an idea is almost so easy, it feels somewhat naughty...

SECRET 26
TAKE A BUSINESS IDEA FROM ANOTHER INDUSTRY

This technique sounds like I'm about to recommend 'industrial espionage'. Well, not quite, no need for wire tapping or going through anyone's bins with this one (sure you'll be delighted to hear that).

In fact, this beautifully simple, and yet rarely used method is another brilliant way of being stimulated to come up with your version of something already existing.

When you're chasing any goal, it's easy to get completely immersed in the subject area it's related to. As we've established, a large degree of *focus* is vital to get a job done and to become great at doing that task. However, sometimes that same focus can blind us to opportunities from the outside – and these opportunities can be hugely valuable. So, this technique once again reinforces the huge importance of 'jump starting' your brain. Thus…

YOU CAN ONLY BE INSPIRED
IF WHAT YOU EXPERIENCE IS INSPIRING

When you're actively trying to come up with a new idea, you must feed your brain with inputs that spark it to start thinking along interesting routes. Only when you feed your imagination will it flourish.

With this technique, you start by looking at what other industries or people are doing OUTSIDE of the sector your goal is in, and then take their success (or failure) and use it as the basis for your new ideas. You can either take an outsider's *process*, *marketing idea* or even *product* as your starting point. All that matters is that your brain is triggered by something from a source not normally found in the area that your task occupies.

A very simple, literal example of this technique is when I used what was happening in the technology industry to help me dream up a new item for the gift industry.

As you know, the tech giant Apple has released many successful products, one of them being the multi-million selling 'iPad', a product that single-handedly revolution-ised the 'tablet computer' market. Now, when the iPad was launched with huge fanfare, I watched with keen interest. As I saw how well it sold and watched the iPad become a global phenomenon, I began to admire this success and see if I could apply anything about its meteoric rise to the gift industry. And that's the pivotal part to this technique – not only to identify a success from an industry outside yours, but also to give that success a little bit of thought so that you can examine the processes involved. This will be sure to help you with your 'Eureka' moment.

EUREKA!

As soon as I started to think along these lines, a simple idea immediately popped into my head: I'd make a product that looked exactly like the iPad but made entirely of paper and call it the 'iNotePad'. Not only would it be a fun gift, it'd be a functional, useful notepad, too.

So, I contacted a talented graphic designer I'd worked with in the past and, after we'd agreed on the look of the new notepad, I sent the designs to China. While I was getting the first samples of the pad made, I took great care to ensure that the top of the notepad was covered with a thin clear acetate sheet, so that the finished pad would look like it had a reflective screen, just like the original object I was parodying. It actually took a long time to get the acetate sheet to sit correctly on the pad, and during the frustrating months of me having samples sent back and forth from China, I frequently found myself questioning why a so-called 'adult male' (i.e. me) cared so much about a plastic sheet on a novelty notepad.

But, actually, the principle of caring about the experience of every 'end user' is totally vital to success in any area, whether you're making a novelty product, trying to get a job, finding a life partner or running a company.

Within a few months, we'd finally conquered the challenges with the acetate sheet and I'd also made the decision to increase the thickness of the backboard, which the pad was stuck onto, so it made the whole notepad very rigid and stiff – again, to mimic the real life electronic aluminium-cased iPad.

As you know, I believe 'details' like this are crucially important in anything you do – they're what connect you to your audience and make the difference between you having a large or small success. And most people – or customers – gravitate towards people or companies who *care* about what they offer or produce.

WHEN YOU 'SWEAT THE SMALL STUFF...' PEOPLE NOTICE AND APPRECIATE IT

Now, on the day my finished notepads arrived, I was elated. But there were some unexpected circumstances that soon emerged. The events that would play out were not only comedic and slightly tragic, they also neatly prove that even huge challenges can be overcome by some quick thinking and good intentions.

One day, soon after my iNotePads arrived from China, I received a letter from a highly respected – and enormous – legal firm. I opened it to discover that the letter was to inform me that Apple Corp (yes, *the* Apple Corp) were objecting to two features on my new novelty notepad. My reaction was a mixture of excitement and fear as I realised I was now on the radar of the world's biggest company, or at least their legal team, anyway.

The letter explained that the objections to my notepad were about the name that I had on the top of pad – 'iNotePad' – and also to the logo that I placed on the back, just above the brand name 'Nice Pear'. It was the silhouette of a pear with a bite mark out of it and a leaf on the top.

I called up the law firm and asked them if they were serious about having issues with my novelty notepad. Unfortunately, they were. The lawyer told me that Apple believed that the fact that I had the letter 'i' and 'Pad' in the same title infringed their copyright. He continued to tell me that my 'Nice Pear' logo contained a 'bite mark' and 'a leaf' graphic that were proprietary to Apple as well. It seemed my parody was just a little too close.

The law firm then sent me a thick document that charted the various incarnations of the Apple logo through the years since the company began. It was actually a really thrilling document to see – a piece of cultural memorabilia in a way. But after I'd *'ooohed'* and *'ahhhed'* over all the meticulous graphics and vintage documentation, I had to come back down to Earth and deal with the fact that a multi-billion dollar company had a legal problem with my novelty notepad.

So, I started a series of discussions with the legal team and, instead of hiring (expensive) legal counsel myself, I simply informed the Apple lawyers about my modest wish to make a juvenile notepad both spoofing and paying homage to their wonderful leap forward in computer hardware. They understood that my paper notepad wasn't in danger of damaging sales of their real iPad – and I, in turn, understood that they had certain trademarks that were important to them.

In the end, after many very civil conversations, we came up with a solution that we were all happy with: I'd change both the name of my product to 'NotPad' and alter the shape of the 'Nice Pear' logo so that it didn't have a bite mark. Plus, I'd also change the shape of the leaf graphic and make my logo consist of two pears instead of one (which was actually even better, given I was still going to use the spoof name 'Nice Pear'). The new 'Notpads' sold hugely well, and swiftly became a smash hit around the world.

Now, there are quite a few important points here. I'm sure that if I'd told a selection of people about my plans for my pad, they might have been 'Negnets', and told me (quite rightly) that Apple might object, and that I shouldn't proceed. If I'd listened to that (reasonable) feedback, I would have stopped right then and nothing more would have happened. I would have had no big challenges, but I'd have missed out on both the adventure and the success too. Instead, as soon as I had the idea, I bounded on doggedly, and came out the other end smelling of…well…

APPLES

(Sorry.)

The other important point of this experience is that even this small example from my life neatly shows that there's usually always a solution to any hurdles you encounter. So, while it's prudent to think of a W.C.S. (worst case scenario) before you throw yourself into making something happen, you should be very wary of not trying something because of future problems you think might occur. What you won't know at that point is whether those problems will *definitely* occur – or whether you'll be able to overcome them if they do. When you do eventually encounter any hurdles, you simply have to power on and either discuss any challenges sensibly or figure out workable ways around the problems you're facing.

The good news is that you'll often find that your great brain – and the great brains of the people you're dealing with, will come up with solutions that neatly dodge the hurdles or make them disappear entirely.

SECRET 27
WHAT'S YOUR BOILED EGG?

This is an unusual one, but I hope you'll still like it. During a trip to the fabulous city of San Francisco, I happened to walk into a corner store and saw something that both surprised and inspired me.

As I approached the counter to buy a bottle of orange juice, I noticed something that really didn't fit in. Now, this store was a completely typical general store, selling everything you'd expect – from candy bars to groceries to gossip magazines, and every single item was professionally produced and packaged by an outside company, except one, and that's why it caught my eye...

There, sitting on the counter, was a small, rather pretty wicker basket and in it sat half a dozen beautiful white eggs, still in their shells. On the side of the basket was a crude, handwritten piece of paper that displayed a price – $0.40 EA.

Quite apart from my initial amusement at seeing a well-known saying come to life in brilliant three-dimension (*'Don't put all your eggs in one basket'*), I was baffled as to why this was the only offering in the shop that was clearly handmade (out of thousands of highly polished commercial goods that packed the store). I'd already seen branded and professionally packaged eggs in the fridge at the back of the shop when I went to select my drink, so what on earth was this odd collection of shells doing on the front counter?

'IT'S NOT EVEN EASTER!'

So, I asked the shopkeeper, *'What are those?'* And the story he told me fascinated me. *'They're hard-boiled eggs,'* he said. He must have noticed the micro-expression of bewilderment that flashed across my face, because he continued to explain: *'There's a gym around the corner and a lot of the fitness fanatics come in and have a boiled egg before or after a workout – it's great protein.'* I processed this information, and then continued to ask him about the eggs, stuttering slightly. *'What? Wow…So, you boil these eggs yourself and then put them in a basket and charge forty cents to the gym-goers?'* I said, double-checking, captivated by this wildly entrepreneurial act *'Yeah…it wasn't my idea…'* the shopkeeper continued. *'The guy I bought the store from used to do it…so I carried on.'*

'Oh wow, that's amazing!' I replied. *'How did that come about?'* I asked, half to the shop owner and half to myself.

The guy didn't know how the 'boiled-egg basket' had actually started, and it got me thinking. At some point, the previous shopkeeper must have gone through quite a few clever thought processes. He might have thought something like this:

'HMMM…I KNOW THERE'S A GYM NEARBY…AND A LOT OF MY CUSTOMERS ARE MEMBERS OF THAT GYM…SOME OF THEM WILL WANT A FAST, FRESH, HEALTHY HIT OF PROTEIN – AN EGG COULD DO THAT…BUT I'LL NEED TO BOIL THE EGGS…AND THEN DISPLAY THEM…SO I WILL…'

Or, very much more likely, the 'boiled-egg basket' came about when someone who visited the gym came into the store one day and asked *'Have you got a boiled egg?'* and, after enquiring why the person wanted a boiled egg, the shopkeeper must have replied, *'No, but I'll have one for you tomorrow!'* That night, the shopkeeper must have taken the thoughtful step of boiling one or two eggs for that customer. That was the first clever step he took.

CRUCIALLY though, the shopkeeper must have then taken another inspired – and important – leap, by deciding to predict that other gym-goers might like a boiled egg too. So, at that point, he must have started selling them in a basket on his counter. And, because the eggs sold – just like that, the shopkeeper created a brand new 'product' for a selection of future customers who might never have asked for it were it not now existing. And what was also amazing was that this new 'product' went down so well with its target market that the shopkeeper who later bought the store was still carrying on this practice of boiling the eggs and putting them in a basket, every single day.

For me, this is a wonderfully exciting example of *entrepreneurialism*. It also brings to life two very helpful 'success mantras' in a beautifully clear way:

ALWAYS BE LOOKING FOR NEW OPPORTUNITIES

BE SENSITIVE TO PEOPLE'S NEEDS

The shopkeeper had not only CARED about his original customer (he was sensitive enough to bother boiling an egg or two for the original gym-goer), he'd also then had the presence of mind to consider whether other fitness fanatics would also love a boiled egg as well.

NOT ONLY WAS THE SHOPKEEPER
OPEN AND RECEPTIVE TO PEOPLE'S NEEDS
HE TOOK THOSE NEEDS AND TURNED THEM INTO
A BUSINESS OPPORTUNITY

Now, of course, selling seven boiled eggs a day will never make you rich or get you on the front cover of *Time* magazine (if those are even noble aims), but what the shopkeeper did was exciting – and important – in two ways: first, he made a certain group of people's lives slightly better by giving them something they wanted; and, second, he created a solid, undeniable new business opportunity.

For me, making people's lives better and creating new opportunities are most definitely very worthwhile outcomes, plus they're vital parts of creating successful and fulfilling lives for every one of us.

So, it's always good to be looking for opportunities around you and for ways to deliver something that people want. And soon, you may very well find your next 'boiled egg'…

SECRET 28
THE A.S.I.A. METHOD

When I decide to start something new, I always go through a mental filter that helps me decide which of my ideas I should tackle first. Like you, maybe, I have lots of ideas and sometimes it's hard to know in which order to start making them happen.

Now, I use a simple technique and it's based upon the knowledge I've built up that...

MAKING ANYTHING HAPPEN WILL MEAN YOU ENCOUNTER HURDLES

Other words for 'hurdles' in this situation are 'roadblocks', 'setbacks', 'crisis points', 'aggravation' and 'stress'! In short, there will always be challenges you have to overcome in order to bring your idea to life. Every single person encounters these. It's certainly not easy starting something new, but boy, it's worth it!

Because hurdles will always exist when you decide to make an idea happen, it makes it slightly easier to decide which of your ideas you should start first, because in order to reach that goal, the THOUGHT of the goal has to excite you so wildly that this excitement will give you the energy to overcome any hurdles that might appear on the journey ahead.

This is really important.

For me, a lot of my life has simply been about trying to make ideas happen because the mere thought of finishing those ideas completely and utterly lights my fire. And this FIRE is what helps melt away the cold, hard barriers that always occur along the road to success. Most of the ideas I decide to pursue aren't driven by the desire to make money. Although, if the thought of making tons of cash floats your boat, then get in and start rowing, of course.

The important point is that, in order to gain the energy to tackle challenges you'll face along the way to any goal, you need to carefully choose which goals you start actioning. You need to check with yourself that any goal you choose to follow is something that fills you with the highest amount of joy and excitement when you think about completing it.

Now, once I've decided what goal I want to tackle, I try to stick to a set of rules for how to engage people with what I'm doing, and these rules oddly spell the word 'ASIA'.

So, here are my A.S.I.A. rules for how to make sure that anything you do captures someone's attention and engages them, so that you'll be hugely successful.

AMAZE

SHOCK

INFORM

AMUSE

These rules should really be applied to ANY creative or business endeavour. If you're not doing at least ONE of these four, then it's likely you're just repeating something that's gone before and people won't notice or engage with it. So, if you use the A.S.I.A. checklist, it'll give you the best shot at having people notice what you're doing.

SECRET 29
THE ART OF CHUNKING

No, it's not a new form of martial art. 'Chunking' is a simple technique I use whenever I'm facing a mammoth goal I want to tackle.

When you're faced with completing a big task, it often seems overwhelming to start it and very easy to decide not to bother. One way you can get the boost necessary to spur you on is to constantly focus on the thought of reaching your desired end result, visualising it in your mind and savouring the way that feels. This should help you overcome any challenges along the way.

As well as doing this, it's a great idea to break up an enormous goal into smaller, more manageable chunks, because then it becomes much less daunting – and therefore seems much more achievable, which allows you to start tackling it. And the key to this 'chunking' process is to reward yourself in some small way after you've completed every little chunk.

In my case, writing this book presented me with one such situation. For me, completing a book is a tough task that's not a natural skill for me. Even though the thought of creating something useful for you that hopefully you'll enjoy, engage with and get good use from, *does* most definitely wildly excite me, there are still DOZENS of things I'd rather be doing – and could be doing – than sitting at my computer writing away.

So, in order to get the job done, I use a simple technique:

TINY TARGETS AND SMALL REWARDS

By setting myself the task of writing a small part of the book every day, in fact, just one page a day, then the job gets done slowly, bit by bit. Then, the task at hand doesn't seem so overwhelming, which is very helpful, because if an ambition or goal seems so far off or unmanageable, it's easy to convince yourself that it's not achievable and to listen to the demon voices in your head that say *'Don't bother starting, the end goal is so far off, you'll most likely never finish…'* It's vital to recognise those demon voices as soon as they appear and employ strategies that help diminish them.

If you set your mini-targets really low, then each one won't seem such a mountain to climb because it won't be that much of a challenge compared with the overall task. Each mini-target then becomes a little hill that you can easily stroll up, and climbing up lots of hills will mean you eventually scale the mountain you're trying to conquer.

For me, I find it's helpful to set these mini-targets astronomically low. Then you'll often find you naturally go over your target anyway, and feel good about yourself – plus it reinforces you shooting for another mini-target again the following day.

The way I spur myself on to complete the mini-target is to plan a small reward for when I complete it. And the reward can change, too. So, in the case of writing this book, every day I write a page, sometimes my reward is to watch a T.V. show I love or sometimes it's a tasty treat that I'll hold off eating until I've finished my mini-target (I adore globe artichokes, for example). On other occasions, I'll tell myself I'll only go out with friends or check my email once I've completed one more page of my book.

This psychological trick helps me give myself enough incentive to complete something that I find a challenge to do. And, gradually, each tiny target gets completed, until the last one is done. Then, your task is complete.

AWESOME!

SECRET 30
THE ULTIMATE SECRET

Okay, brace yourself. Here's the biggest secret to success…

ALL THAT MATTERS IS ACTION

And now for another bold statement: the only way you definitely *won't* achieve anything you desire, is by *not* starting to make those desires happen. My simple assertion to you is that…

ACTION ALWAYS PROVIDES RESULTS

What's marvellous about taking the first step to starting something new (whether that first step is a phone call, some research on the web or speaking to an expert) is that once you start moving forwards towards any goal, your actions will only ever provide two results, both of which are helpful.

The results of trying something new will either be…

A 'DIRECT POSITIVE'

That is, you get what you want *right away* – or (yes, you've guessed it)…

AN 'INDIRECT POSITIVE'

(Which some people would call a 'stumbling block', 'challenge' or even 'failure').

Now, the 'indirect positive' is simply something that tells you what *not* to do in the future, so that's a great learning point isn't it!

It's very important to recognise that any instances where you don't reach your goal straight away, aren't 'end points' (unless you let them be); they are simply markers along the way to help you achieve what you want. They are not 'failures' – and you're not 'failing' at all, because of this one true fact:

YOU'RE ACTUALLY 'LEARNING ON YOUR PATH TO SUCCESS'

You'll only 'fail' if you don't use what you experience to alter your behaviour next time you move towards your target. In fact, you'll find that by simply moving forwards, the most incredible things start to happen. Even if you don't immediately reach your goal, you'll definitely learn things that will help you get there eventually, plus surprising opportunities may well arise from your actions. And these opportunities can often take you in yet more exciting directions.

I believe in the concept of…

This idea comes from the expression:

**'THROW ENOUGH MUD AT THE WALL
AND EVENTUALLY SOME OF IT WILL STICK'**

The fact of the matter is this…as long as you keep trying lots of new things – or even trying to reach one particular goal doggedly enough (using different strategies along the way) – some of your mud will *definitely* 'stick to the wall'. You just have to start throwing, because unless you're throwing some mud, nothing can ever stick.

Start something new

Starting something new is the hardest thing of all.

You will not be brilliant at it the first time you do something new. So, armed with this knowledge, you can now relax…and then challenge yourself to see how well you can do things first time.

Plus, it's comforting to realise that when you start something new, you're starting off a thrilling chain of events:

Once you start doing something…

You will get SOME results the first time you try…

You'll get BETTER results the second time…

You'll get EVEN MORE BRILLIANT results the tenth time.

Because…

YOU ARE A LEARNING MACHINE

So you're pretty much guaranteed to always get better.

When I decided to become a novelty product designer, one of my biggest ambitions was to get a product into the trendy worldwide chain of gift stores, Urban Outfitters. I created a range of birthday candles that displayed cheeky slogans like 'You're Old', 'Lost Count' and 'Don't Ask'. I teamed up with a superb company to bring the candles to glorious life, but Urban Outfitters told us they didn't want to stock them and I was hugely disappointed. They said that the candles wouldn't be popular enough. Then, unbeknownst to me the candles were considered for 'Gift Of The Year', a respected industry award. I was both amazed and delighted when it was announced that my 'You're Old' candles had won the 'Hot Novelty' category. This then brought the range to the forefront and they were seen as a successful product by the gift industry. Plus, it gave them an extra kudos that they didn't previously have. The candles started to sell in huge numbers, topping over a quarter of a million units. And – yes – you guessed it – after the award, the whole range was accepted and sold by Urban Outfitters.

So, this is a great example of how if you decide to make something happen, not only will it take you on a great adventure, it could also make you money too. Plus, if you keep going through any challenges you encounter, you'll often get exactly what you set out to do at the start. And what's completely vital to remember is that the beginning of any success you have will always start with a *thought*…

PEOPLE OFTEN SAY
'IT'S THE "THOUGHT" THAT COUNTS'

'THE THOUGHT' IS IMPORTANT, YES…

BUT IT'S THE ACTION AFTER THE THOUGHT
THAT REALLY COUNTS…

AND THAT'S WHY WE ALL JUST NEED
TO START SOMETHING!

SUCCESSFULLY YOURS...

So, that's all from me. Thanks for your time...

I hope you've enjoyed this book and found it useful. If you did, please leave a review on Amazon (the reviews submitted there are HUGELY powerful – and enormously appreciated too) and do let your friends and family know about this book as well...

THANK YOU!

Now, maybe go begin something you've been thinking about doing for ages.

I wish you all the success in the world...

Shed x

Please add me on Twitter, Facebook or LinkedIn

CHARLATANS OF THE WORLD UNITE
WE HAVE NOTHING TO LOSE BUT OUR FAÇADES

SUCCESS...OR YOUR MONEY BACK...

I'm a man of my word, so if – after reading this book and implementing the ideas within it – you feel you'd like your money back, simply film a video of yourself with your copy of the book, talking about how you used the techniques inside and describing the success you want to achieve.

Upload your video to YouTube with the title 'Success Or Your Money Back' and your name in the title too, and send an email to:

video@successoryourmoneyback.com

...so we know it's there. We'll then watch your video and get in touch with you as soon as we can...

First published and distributed in the United Kingdom by:
Hay House UK Ltd, 292B Kensal Rd, London W10 5BE. Tel.: (44) 20 8962 1230;
Fax: (44) 20 8962 1239. www.hayhouse.co.uk

Published and distributed in the United States of America by:
Hay House, Inc., PO Box 5100, Carlsbad, CA 92018-5100. Tel.: (1) 760 431 7695 or
(800) 654 5126; Fax: (1) 760 431 6948 or (800) 650 5115.
www.hayhouse.com

Published and distributed in Australia by:
Hay House Australia Ltd, 18/36 Ralph St, Alexandria NSW 2015. Tel.: (61) 2 9669
4299; Fax: (61) 2 9669 4144. www.hayhouse.com.au

Published and distributed in the Republic of South Africa by:
Hay House SA (Pty), Ltd, PO Box 990, Witkoppen 2068. Tel./Fax: (27) 11 467 8904.
www.hayhouse.co.za

Published and distributed in India by:
Hay House Publishers India, Muskaan Complex, Plot No.3, B-2, Vasant Kunj,
New Delhi – 110 070. Tel.: (91) 11 4176 1620; Fax: (91) 11 4176 1630.
www.hayhouse.co.in

Distributed in Canada by:
Raincoast, 9050 Shaughnessy St, Vancouver, BC V6P 6E5.
Tel.: (1) 604 323 7100; Fax: (1) 604 323 2600

Text © Shed Simove, 2012

The moral rights of the author have been asserted.

Hello, I'm the Copyright Page. I'm not the most riveting page ever found in a book,
but I'm vitally important in the wonderful world of publishing. The fact that you're
reading me means you're an independent and quirky thinker who looks in unusual
places for information, which is a great start if you're a person who likes to make
things happen, because having an enquiring mind and being able to make discoveries
in places where not everyone would search, are hugely important traits for anyone
who's going to be successful in everything they do.
So hats off to you and LOVING your work!
The Copyright Page (and Shed) x

A catalogue record for this book is available from the British Library.

ISBN 978-1-84850-974-0
Interior images: p.i photographer: Tom Banfield

MIX
Paper from
responsible sources
FSC
www.fsc.org FSC® C013056

Printed and bound in Great Britain by TJ International, Padstow, Cornwall.